MW00896854

Meditations of a Madman

Meditations of a Madman

The Musings of a Hated Man Loving God

dna

Love God deliberately!

Brian K. Woodson, Sr.

Copyright © 2006 by Brian K. Woodson, Sr.

ISBN: Softcover   1-4257-1166-9

All rights reserved. No part of this book may be reproduced or transmitted in any form or by any means, electronic or mechanical, including photocopying, recording, or by any information storage and retrieval system, without permission in writing from the copyright owner.

Scripture quotations marked (CEV) are from the Contemporary English Version Copyright © 1991, 1992, 1995 American Bible Society, Used by Permission.

All other scriptures are from the King James Version.

Cover design by Lance A. Pettiford.

This book was printed in the United States of America.

To order additional copies of this book, contact:
Xlibris Corporation
1-888-795-4274
www.Xlibris.com
Orders@Xlibris.com
31946

To love God desperately while being hated openly
can only be gently lived in madness.

Dedication

To those who both helped me and hurt me, though I often misunderstood your intentions: I dedicate this book with my deepest thanks. All of you were tools Christ used to shape me into the person he desired me to be.

Meditations of a Madman:
The Musings of a Hated Man Loving God

Foreword

Presupposition

Meditations of a Madman:
The Musings of a Hated Man Loving God

Meditations of a Madman:
The Musings of a Hated Man Loving God

I am moved by Reverend Woodson's words that Jesus annulled the orthodoxy of his day by offering a fresh interpretation of Moses and the Hebrew scriptures. This is precisely what Pastor Woodson does with the theology and biblical interpretations of the contemporary church. He finds fresh meanings and new treasures from the sacred scriptures.

The vivacity of Professor Woodson's words, the clarity of his images, the carefulness of his thoughts, and the beauty of his writing, gives to this book a symphonic beauty. Along with his stylish prose is a depth of theological utterance that captivates the mind. I refer to the following moving sentences from Reverend Woodson's book: "Heaven's Christ is not beyond us to be longed for but among us to be realized." "Esther participated with Providence and won a place in the admiration of her people and the canon." And "Actors at the altar of the Almighty sacrifice their souls and accumulate the utter disdain of the Divine." These meditations speak with prophetic challenge and devotional sensitivity.

Thanks be to God for Brian Woodson, Sr., his life and ministry, and above all this very moving and well-written book that is designed to guide us along life's journey on the road that honors God and uplifts humankind.

Prayerfully,

J. Alfred Smith

J. Alfred Smith, Sr.
Senior Pastor, Allen Temple Baptist Church
And
Distinguished Professor of Preaching and Church Ministries,
The American Baptist Seminary of the West and
The Graduate Theological Union, Berkeley, California

FOREWORD

Not every book challenges me. Some books are hard to read. Others are shallow in meaning, ones that authors write merely to say that they have written and published a book. But Brian Woodson, Sr., has written very eloquently about things that matter the most. His depth of expression reveals the beauty of the mansions of his mind. He is a classic thinker whose thoughts are dyed with the colors of spiritual beauty.

Students of Howard Thurman and Martin Luther King, Jr., will discover in reading Meditations of a Madman that God speaks with power through Professor Woodson's inspiring and enlightening writings. I call him Professor Woodson because he teaches Religious Studies at the Leadership Institute of Allen Temple Baptist Church of Oakland, California. He is well loved by his students and his classes are crowded with their young, hungry minds. In my efforts to reacquaint myself with Biblical Hebrew, Reverend Woodson was my tutor. For many weeks, we read from The Hebrew Bible and Pastor Woodson helped me to see truths there that are hidden in the English Bible.

I am amazed that a person of Pastor Woodson's depth is so humble and down to earth. He is kind enough to reveal his goodness and his humility. His meditations touch each of us who struggle with the challenges of life. If you want to grow as a person, and if you are searching for the relevance of sacred scriptures for living victoriously in our age of cynicism and skepticism, a daily study of Meditations of a Madman will help you in your quest.

I am moved by Reverend Woodson's words that Jesus annulled the orthodoxy of his day by offering a fresh interpretation of Moses and the Hebrew scriptures. This is precisely what Pastor Woodson does with the theology and biblical interpretations of the contemporary church. He finds fresh meanings and new treasures from the sacred scriptures.

The vivacity of Professor Woodson's words, the clarity of his images, the carefulness of his thoughts, and the beauty of his writing, gives to this book a symphonic beauty. Along with his stylish prose is a depth of theological utterance that captivates the mind. I refer to the following moving sentences from Reverend Woodson's book: "Heaven's Christ is not beyond us to be longed for but among us to be realized." "Esther participated with Providence and won a place in the admiration of her people and the canon." And "Actors at the altar of the Almighty sacrifice their souls and accumulate the utter disdain of the Divine." These meditations speak with prophetic challenge and devotional sensitivity.

Thanks be to God for Brian Woodson, Sr., his life and ministry, and above all this very moving and well-written book that is designed to guide us along life's journey on the road that honors God and uplifts humankind.

Prayerfully,

J. Alfred Smith, Sr.
Senior Pastor, Allen Temple Baptist Church
And
Distinguished Professor of Preaching and Church Ministries,
The American Baptist Seminary of the West and
The Graduate Theological Union, Berkeley, California

The Presupposition

I am convinced that Jesus encouraged the people who gathered around him not just to believe but to think. There may have been literate members of the community in Jesus' day with the ability to read and interpret the holy writings of the Torah or the contemporary thoughts of others. But, most of the information needed to form systems of faith and religious beliefs was communicated through songs, storytelling, and the superstitious laden interpretations of observed and reported events. Proper religious conduct then was demonstrated and informed by the leader of each group or the person one sought out for guidance. Into this orthodoxy, Jesus comes, smashing the then prevailing notions of God and righteousness. Moses and the Hebrew cannon had come to be understood and practiced in an orthodoxy that Jesus annulled. This is why so often in the New Testament the religious leaders and Jesus seem at odds. Jesus took the Hebrew Scriptures and shook from them the important understandings of God's nature. He separated the life lessons that were relevant to the present from the instructions to people in the past. This, too, is our task. First, we must think, not just believe. It is more important to know why we believe than it is to know what we believe. Then we must extract God's message to us in our present state from the instructions to people in the past.

This book is an exploration of Christian faith, a discussion of what should be believed and thought today using the Bible as the guide. Because of how I am wired mentally, I need centering, contemplative time in the morning or my day will spin in a cacophony of activity, and I will loose the music of my soul. Without these moments, I wind up wearing a mask of pleasant peace and happiness over a melancholy malaise that increasingly grips my hopes and darkens my thoughts. The thoughts captured on these pages rose from these morning meditations. The task of these morning moments was not only to quiet my mind but also to discern the reality of Christ and his requirements in the midst of this present context. It is this life of struggling to find real godly peace and purpose that has brought these pages into being.

I believe the mind is the synthesis of all it receives. We cannot study or think or live in a vacuum; rather, while we are studying, thinking, and living our minds are processing and filtering innumerable stimuli, most of which we remain unaware. This is true of my contemplative moments. I would sit in quiet stillness reading the Bible in search of my daily connection with the Divine and my mind would still reverberate with emotions, perspectives, and memories of which I was barely conscious. Then a text would spark and set a thought on fire in my mind. My only way of extinguishing the sorrow, rage, or raw emotion blazing in my conscious was to write. So the passages presented in these pages come to you not as the result of an attempt to write a book but as a record of moments when the Bible came alive to me. These passages were born as mental and emotional outbursts. I transcribed them to paper so that they would no longer scream in my mind. The passages are not complete theological expositions. And I do not offer them with my defense. Rather, I encourage you to read them as they came to me in the midst of contemplative time, considering what the God of the Bible has to say today to you in your context and to the world you know. I encourage you to read these passages in conjunction with your own Bible study, and may we wrestle together until Christ is clear to us in this everlasting present.

I want to live well and die blissfully aware of my departure. Faith in Christ is central for me to live this life God and I mutually agree we want, a life that is filled with peace and seasoned with pleasure. To live well is to live a life that is a blessing and benefit to others. I believe this is what Christ means when he said he came "that we might have life and that more abundantly." As a protestant and Pastor, I believe that the richest source of wisdom for living such a life is the Bible. But I struggle with just how these ancient fragments of Christ's life and the religious history of an otherwise historically insignificant people can speak to me. What follows are accounts of encounters with the word of God in the context of my experience. For me they are glimpses of God in my mind. Thoughts that rise from a living document, an ancient mirror that still reflects the love and wisdom of a God who would send his son to die for strangers like you . . . and me.

This work would not exist without the continued love and support of my wife Valerie McCann Woodson who creates with her gentleness a safe place for a madman to emote and grow. And these pages would have remained bits in my laptop without the professional and prescriptive assistance of Laureece Hymes who bridled raw enthusiasm and energy into something tangible. I bow beneath the grace of God and thank the Almighty for Clara A. Moore Woodson and Edwin Woodson, Jr., mom and dad, who remain the fire from which the metal of my mind was forged. I thank Dr. J. Alfred Smith, Sr. who has taught me more about preaching, being a pastor, and living as a man of God than any other teacher. He continues to inspire me to nobility and is my greatest mentor. And I would have remained unsure of many things were it not for the precise and guiding eye of my friend Dr. David Nystrom. To all the family, church members and friends of this man and mind I thank you for the inspiration and help you have given. And finally to all who read this work may good thoughts reign always in your mind.

Meditations of a Madman:

The Musings of a Hated Man Loving God

Jesus wept.
John 11:35

Death is the door through which all living must pass. It is a portal through which those of us who cling to this life may peer, but never pass. It is a dark glass reflecting an image of ourselves distorted by sadness and corrupted by grief. Yet our tears are a witness of something wonderful, and our pains, with their particular expressions, are provoked by the privilege of our past. If we had not loved, we would not hurt. If our heart had not been opened and caressed by love's gentle embrace, we would not weep.

Jesus is at the tomb of Lazarus, a dear friend. The deceased is survived by two sisters, Mary and Martha. Jesus loved all three of them. And the three of them loved Jesus. Mary, called a sinner by those who opposed Jesus, once washed Jesus' feet with her tears and expensive perfume, drying them with her hair. She was the woman who sat at Jesus' feet and was instructed by him as he taught in her home. Martha engaged her friendship with energy. She cooked and cared for Jesus when he visited and today has run to meet the healer, who was delayed on the road to her house. Days earlier, Jesus had been summoned to the bedside of his ailing friend. But, for reasons he knew and we do not, he tarried and Lazarus died. For four days Lazarus lied motionless, breathless and cold. For four days the hope of salvation from death's sorrow diminished. Eventually, the motionless carcass was carried to the grave and cast lovingly into a tomb. A stone was set and sealed at its entrance signifying the end of hope for Lazarus in this life. Jesus arrives and the triumph of sorrow is consummated as the master of life and death weeps. Jesus loved Lazarus. Jesus loved the people broken by grief. Now death and sorrow have broken his heart, and the maker and master of the universe weeps.

God softens hearts by breaking them. To misunderstand this is to tempt tyranny; it is to propagate justice in the name of a righteousness that is without compassion. We learn to love others by desperately realizing the need to be loved ourselves. The soul of compassion is to see our own hopes flickering in the darkening eyes of another. The heart of deep love is to fan to flames the flickering hopes of one lost to love's warm embrace.

The impotent man answered him, Sir I have no man,
when the water is troubled, to put me in the pool . . .
John 5:7

Often the world is viewed as full of forces beyond our control, which affect our future and fortune. Wind, storm, and rain bring their sunshine, flowers, and pain—all without our input or personal desires. Our lives can be viewed as tumble weeds dried, tossed, and driven by disinterested forces completely beyond our control or influence.

Jesus is walking through the city of Jerusalem and notices a man among a sea of men incarcerated in the inoperative frame of human flesh. The man is impotent and crippled and had been so for thirty-eight years. Thirty-eight years is a lifetime for some and enough time for most to have given up, yet this man remains waiting for an opportunity to be changed. What Jesus sees within him, we do not know. Why Jesus seeks and speaks to this one among so many, we can't say. But the story tells that Jesus initiates this meeting between God and man, between the need and the supply, and in so doing extinguishes excuses that keep so many of us impotent beside the pool, instead of active in our lives and in the drama of God. Jesus speaks and confronts the very substance of the man's presence at the pool with the question, "Do you want to be well?" It is a question which dissipates presupposition. The

answer appears first as obfuscation, an attempt perhaps to reestablish the
orthodox paradigm of human impotence in the presence of divine imperative.
This man, on behalf of every man, avoids the direct question and reveals our
unquestioned presupposition with his statement, "I have no man, when the
water is troubled." Here appear two mountainous myths which Jesus soon
dispels. The first is that our access to the source of our hopes, prayers, and
pleas rest on the whims of nature. It is a suggestion that circumstance, with its
often chaotic order, rules in the affairs of our lives. Second is that our deepest
needs will remain unfulfilled without the access to and input of others.

But Christ has declared that the power to move beyond paradigms of
pain, life's paradoxes, and the pressures of personhood lies within us. God
has hidden within the hearts of humanity the gift that exceeds the gratuitous
calamities and approbations of our lives. So . . . live.

And he said, You asked a hard thing: nevertheless,
if you see me when I am taken from you, it will be so to you:
but if not, it will not be so.
2 Kings 2:10

Hidden in every human heart is a divine dream. This dream is a gift to the world and a calling through crucible to the one who holds it. A pilgrimage is a journey to a place you cannot get to by traveling. A quest is the hunger to achieve some goal, which provides the direction within which the pilgrimage occurs. Our life's journey is a pilgrimage. Our life's hope is a quest. Both are burdens to bring to life the dream, which is our calling.

Elisha had been found of him for whom his heart had searched. Years before, Elijah, the great prophet of God, had found Elisha plowing the barren field in hope and preparation of some future harvest. When Elijah met him, he threw his mantle around the plowing prophet-to-be, and Elisha immediately responded to the challenge. Elisha sacrificed the very oxen he had driven moments before and boiled their flesh over a fire kindled with the yoke of their labor. During the years that followed, Elisha became the shadow of the great prophet, ministering to his needs and easing the prophetic burden by bearing the daily tasks of living. But now Elijah, having received a divine and individual invitation to dine at the table of God, desired to walk alone into the dimension of the Almighty. But he could not shake his shadow. Elijah, in exasperation, asks what the young prophet desired to release him to his reward, and Elisha asks for twice the prophetic power and presence of his teacher. Elijah replies positively but conditionally. If you see me when I am taken, you will have your desire; if you do not, you will not. So now Elisha faces the final challenge of his initiation into the mystical and prophetic office of his predecessor. He must keep his eyes open and remain at the side of his mentor until separated by God Almighty.

Godly power to work miracles and walk in wisdom and integrity does not come cheap. There must be an initial investment that comes at a personal cost, just to begin the journey. This is followed by time spent in the shadow of obscurity, where you minister to a cause greater than your own name, a dark place where the seed of greatness can grow. Finally, you must pass the test of divine separation. This is the quest and the pilgrimage, which leads to the only real life there is.

*While Peter thought on the vision, the Spirit said unto him,
Behold three men seek thee.*
Acts 10:19

There is a proclivity of those who would rule to segregate and homogenize. There is a flaw in the untamed human heart to tear against the unfamiliar, to denigrate the alien and even destroy those who are thus disenfranchised.

For three years Jesus taught his disciples that the Kingdom of God encompasses more than the small band of self-identified children of Israel. During these years of daily and divine instruction, Peter was given individual lessons and was clearly identified as one of Christ's closest disciples and best students. Peter was taken to the mount of transfiguration. He was called into the room for the private healing of Jairus's daughter. He was present when Jesus embraced those children who before had been excluded from an audience with the divine. Peter saw the Master's acceptance of the Samaritan woman and could read what Jesus wrote in the sand as the naked adulteress found salvation and deliverance. Peter alone walked on the water with Jesus. Yet even he did not understand that Jesus and the kingdom he opened were inclusive. Instead, Peter continued living a segregated life, one dominated by the false notion that the apparent diversity within the human family amounted to substantive difference in the mind of God. It is only when he achieved a spiritual awareness, induced by food deprivation, that he began to understand that the fold of the good shepherd was larger than he imagined, more diverse and entirely inclusive. Faint with hunger, Peter finally found that the Lord was invested and involved with the very foreigners he assumed were fiends and forgotten by the Father.

God loves and is invested in diversity. God allows people to be different in many ways. Our skin, eye, and hair colors are different. Our hopes are different. Our loves are different, and each of us from the vantage point of our individual being has a particular view of the Almighty. We can share our complimentary views and gather ourselves in mosaic images of hope without attempting to destroy those we do not understand. Or in sightless self-centeredness and violence, we can attempt to homogenize humanity. But God has already accepted those rejected by our blindness, which is induced by our inability to love radically and completely.

And God saw that the wickedness of man was great in the earth,
and that every imagination of the thoughts of his heart was
only evil continually. And it repented the Lord that he had
made man on the earth, and it grieved him at his heart.
Genesis 6:5-6

The capacity of the human heart to embrace evil is matched alone by God's wrath. It was the work of evil imbedded in humanity that savagely slaughtered the native population of the Americas as foreign settlers came and killed. This same dark spirit in the human heart created the American slavocracy that maimed, raped, and killed sold and stolen Africans. It was the evil of the human heart that created the death camps of Auschwitz and Dachau to kill Jews. It was evil in the human heart at Sabra and Shatila where the killed became the killers. It was ravaging evil that motivated machete-wielding teenagers to kill in Rwanda. Evil, like the wind, moves unnoticed across the earth and through time until finding welcome hearts to ravage as humanity's depravity rivals the Almighty's sovereignty.

Near the beginning of the human story appears the saga of the flood. God's project on earth had turned from a divine pastoral pedagogy to an adversarial and alienating alliance. The Bible began with the divine walking with humanity in the garden of the world: God and humanity together exploring the creation, appreciating its diversity, and contributing to its longevity. But men began to multiply on the earth and the text moves from the context of a family centered rural paradigm to the complexity of urban community and culture. In the city, the corruption of the human spirit was in full swing. The control and deportment of the people on the planet was left to desire, which grew ever darker. Because the appetite of evil is rapacious and insatiable, its presence is pervasive. Humanity became intoxicated with the evil that penetrated its soul, as reason was replaced by resentment, which in turn grew to an insanity of profane imagination and an orgy of death. The human heart was affected by the affections of alien angelic beings and their depravity embraced a spiritual dimension as their daughters were taken. God's universal gaze fixed on the blue planet and the divine assessment of the human heart determined that judgment was required. Evil had not only informed human action, it had become humanity's hope. And with a teardrop from the Almighty's eye, the world was washed away and the foreign fire of humankind extinguished.

The want of the human heart is a well which evil seeks to fill. Evil is a cancer that prefers the religious but welcomes every host it maims. It is a wild fire on the horizon threatening mothers' hopes and children's laughter. Although it can neither taste nor enjoy the prey upon which it gorges, evil will never stop indulging itself. It is a force always seeking to penetrate the human soul and thrives in societies where it is tolerated or ignored. Although the pain and presence suggest otherwise, God's answer to humanity's evil is neither accommodation nor conversion. God's answer to evil is annihilation and this, in time, we too shall see.

And the ruler of the synagogue answered
with indignation.
Luke 13:14

There must always be boundaries in life. There must always be things you lust after but struggle not to do because you're convinced that God is opposed to them. We grow older and begin to live without the overt oversight of authority and fall into an often subtle pattern of the pursuit of pleasure. Most of these gifts to ourselves are gentle accommodations for our flesh made with affirmations of our intellect and engaged without notice by the world in which we live. Even when we sacrifice or do for someone else, and in so doing act principally to make ourselves feel better about ourselves, we are engaged in an ungodly and character corrupting pursuit of pleasure.

Jesus is in the synagogue teaching. He is expounding a deep truth about repentance and a deeper truth about who is accepted by God. Many of the openly religious people around the Master regarded some as obvious sinners, due to the circumstances of their lives and manner in which they died. They likewise thought of themselves as righteous because of circumstances and the manner in which they lived. Their pursuit of personal piety had brought them to prominence in their places of worship. They had become recognized as examples of godliness and leaders within their religious communities, but Jesus was not impressed. And as the Master taught, expounding truths intended to open hearts and understanding, he stops abruptly and causes all attention to be placed on the crippled woman in their midst. She had been in this condition for eighteen years. And as silence surrounds her and the light of Jesus' attention reaches her soul, the Master speaks to her, touches her, and heals her. One religious leader is indignant. The act and the actor offend him. He rebukes her. Jesus rebukes him. Now all can see, through Jesus' acts, that the one who outwardly appeared as being on the right path was lost, and the one who appeared doomed was heaven bound. The life of this self-righteous man, lived one decision at a time, led to a piety that elevates the person in his own eyes and community but leaves him far from the narrow road of eternal life. On the other hand, the crippled woman's life of struggle, pain, and suffering leads her through the indifference and ire of the community to the presence, healing, and acceptance of Christ.

If you cannot see the particular boundaries God has placed in your present life, and if you never struggle with these boundaries, you are on the broad way. While we live we will be susceptible to the subtle saturation of sin into ourselves. Know two things about the undisciplined and the under-disciplined life: it is a slippery path whose slope increases with the time spent on it and it leads only to utter eternal destruction.

For there fell down many slain, because the war was of God.
And they dwelt in their places until the captivity.
1 Chronicles 5:22

War cannot reveal the will of God, for if God uses warriors to exact Divine will against other men, God's will is dissolved into the will of men.

Among the long genealogical lists that begin the Chronicler's history, we find an account of how the tribes of Ruben, Gad, and half of Manasseh obtained their land. The brief account suggests that 44,760 battle-tested and fierce warriors from the three tribes declared and fought a war against a coalition of indigenous clans, which resulted in these tribes of Israel possessing the land. There is no provocation mentioned where the defeated people earned or deserved the ire of either God or these particular Israelites. The war's purpose as presented here is to possess the property and progeny of these particular people. It enters the biblical text as an ontology of these particular Israelites. The pericope describes a battle and attributes the success of the Israelite warriors over the coalition warriors to God because they cried out to God and trusted in God. This is an unfortunate reading. God here has no independent will, nor does God respond to a self-contained paradigm of law or justice. God simply serves the will of warriors, who happen to have engaged in the destruction of others for their own benefit. The text presents God controlled by avarice and complicit in caprice.

But to attribute the death and destruction of war to the will of God is to contain God in a paradox within the manipulative mind of men, who imagine themselves both victorious and virtuous after they've destroyed life and civility in order to possess what belonged to someone else. It creates a demand where a God of justice acts outside of justice at the behest of those engaged in destruction, simply because of an earnest request. It subjugates the autonomy of the Divine to the whim of mendacious histories and the heart of the warrior.

*And her adversary also provoked her sore, for to make
her fret, because the Lord had shut up her womb . . .
therefore she wept, and did not eat.*
1 Samuel 1:6-7

The silent siren of the soul sends a clarion call from the depths of our being. We must not seek to deaden the sound by satiating our flesh, for it is a cry that God alone can hear and heaven alone can answer.

Hannah is a woman we meet in the midst of great anguish and little hope. In deep sorrow, she has ceased to eat. The first burden we witness her bearing is that of being one of two wives. The construct of a patriarchy itself inures an individual and societal stress, which would require rigorous mental remedy for all and at least passive systemic resistance among its female constituents. But to compound the injustice with bigamy must have left all but the incredibly strong feminine hearts in a desperate straight. And Hannah had an additional strain. We learn that she had been unproductive in the patriarchal paradigm and had not yet given birth to a child. Peninnah, the other wife, perhaps as a response to her own sense of injustice, tormented her rival and used her fertility and Hannah's infertility to berate and belittle. The husband, himself trapped in this world of parody, increases Hannah's personal torment and justifies her external abuse by declaring his preferential treatment of her at the communal table. The catastrophic circumstances are more than her heart can hold at the moment, and in hurt and despair Hannah leaves the table.

We next find Hannah standing before the temple of God. Her life was overwhelmed with burdens, her heart overpowered by hurt, the cup of her hopes broken, and the concomitant causes of grief left her without any means of self-help. In her world there was no remedy, so her problems pushed and presented her before the Almighty and there before the oracle she wept bitterly. Eli the prophet and priest more accustomed to sins of the flesh than sorrow of the heart mistook her spirit's anguish for licentiousness. But God heard her. She proffered no logic or expectation. She presented no reasoned argument or impassioned plan to alleviate her pain. She simply and deeply grieved before God. But her sorrow spoke in a language God understood, accepted, and answered.

The hunger of the soul is far more powerful than the hunger of the flesh; it has the ability to commune with God and move the Almighty. Deep wounds are Divine seeds which have nothing to do with our flesh: embrace them and then bring them to God.

Therefore her plagues will come in one day death and mourning and famine. And she will be utterly burned with fire, for strong is the Lord God who judges her.
Revelation 18:8

Almighty God has neither the need nor desire to share God's own prerogatives or power. What will be already is and has always been. While we spin our perceptions and declare them our reality, God waits and we are caught in the web of our own deceit. At our hands, the impoverished and disenfranchised languish in the refuse of hell-inspired destruction. Our armies triumph. Our generals stand saluting, bright brass gleaming in the sun, flags waving in the bristled breeze above, and all but the Almighty remain unaware of the children's blood that seeps through the soil of hidden graves. The time has come and it will come when God will be forced by our bloody hands . . . to show His own.

The apostle John, exiled to the isle of Patmos, writes of righteousness in the midst of a cruel context. Christianity had been ostracized and separated from Judaism. Belief in the risen Christ had been declared heretical and followers of Christ were castigated in and forced from the synagogue. Christianity could no longer exist under the umbrella of Judaism, which was an authorized religion under Roman rule, and so the persecution began. Domitian's violent soldiers scattered the blood of new believers and the church herself throughout the Roman Empire in a pogrom to eradicate the church and eviscerate her hopes. John, having witnessed the destructive force of Rome on Jerusalem, her people, and the church, codes his message of hope momentarily unveiled in this testament of God's dominion. John wrote Revelation to the people of his time about the people of his time. We read his story as if it were a yet unrevealed mystery and remain blind to its poignant rebuke of extant power. We are Babylon.

No nation lasts forever. No nation imbrued with hegemonic power is righteous. No people invested in the will, myth, process, or progress of such a nation can long stay the hand of Divine justice. We who enjoy the shadows of oppression cannot blind the Divine to our passive participations in the paradigm of destruction. In fact, if we look closely at our selves we will notice that God's justice has already begun and our hearts are failing and our flesh is following as the demands of justice claims our soiled souls.

Suffer me that I may speak;
and after I have spoken, mock on.
Job 21:3

There is an argument you can only have with God. There is a test of wits in which all of us in this world are revealed as witless. There are times when what you know to be true about yourself is utterly disregarded by heaven and mocked by the earth. There are powerful emotional and cerebral realms of pain and anguish produced when you receive that which your whole being believes you do not deserve. In such times, the consolations of your companions are curses. In such times, the might of heaven alone is your hope.

The friends of Job were good friends but better theologians. They gathered around their friend and mourned in silence for days, then they had to speak, but their words of comfort, phrased in perfect theological defenses of the Divine, were thinly veiled attacks on the piety of Job. Attempting to comfort Job without offending heaven, they rationalized their reasoned understanding of God's justice and could only confidently conclude by commending heaven and condemning Job. But Job had searched his clean heart and callused hands. He had embarked on the journey to justify heaven and understand the hell that had become his home, long before the first words of his companions. His friends could only voice arguments Job had already examined. Job attempts to show himself a just victim of inexplicable violence but this just stoked fires of indignation in his friends and encouraged them further in their dark machinations. The more they heard, the less they understood and the more confident they became.

Job and God alone knew the righteousness in which Job worked. Job and God alone knew the integrity of Job's walk. And Job and God alone knew the unrighteousness of the results. So Job turned from his attempt to reason to an acceptance of the irrational and in so doing turned to God. In the times when conversation is fruitless, prayer is most meaningful.

And Jesus went with him; and much people followed him,
and thronged him. And a certain woman . . .
Mark 5:24

Behind the clamor of our thoughts, beneath the chaos of our emotions, amid the cacophony of impulses, hopes, and dreams there must be the still, small whisper of resolve.

When Jesus arrived on the shores of the Galilean sea, the crowds gathered quickly. Here was the man who had become the talk of the territory. Some thought him to be a God-inspired prophet; others believed him to be some sort of sorcerer. But all had heard that in his presence unusual things happened. So they came—no ticket needed—some to see magic, others a miracle; but they all came and crowded around him, each vying to get the best view of what they were sure would be a noteworthy event. But not all in this crowd were passive participants. There was also present a ruler of the synagogue, a man who came not just to see Jesus but to interdict him. This man needed Jesus' particular attention because all the elements of his world had been focused by an event outside his control and beyond his power. He came to Jesus because life had given him the tragic gift of seeing clearly an essential need of his life. His daughter was dying. The love for his daughter and hope for her life diminished all other images. The only hope he had was Jesus, so there, before the crowd he became the object of their curiosity and the scene they had sought, as on his knees he pleaded for the Lord to come with him. But there was another person even more focused than he. It was a woman who for years had been oppressed by a malady that proved itself more powerful than the wisdom of her physicians. The disease had destroyed her finances. It had ruined her faith in medicine and depleted her hope for human help. But the years of torment, the endless hours of despair had brought laser focus to her resolve. She needed the Master. But she did not need to move him or command his attention, she only needed to touch the hem of his garment.

Of all the energies we expend in pursuit of good or gold, which do we count most precious? When we are reduced to our single essential confidence, what do we believe? The crowd thronged him and got nothing. The ruler begged him and got something. The woman touched him and got everything.

*And He did not many mighty works there
because of their unbelief*
Matthew 13:58

It is an awesome and sobering wonder that Almighty God has chosen to be constrained by our small minds and ability to disbelieve what we hear with our own ears and see with our own eyes. There is a subtle and simple choice each of us makes, which either releases the power of Christ in our lives and world or prevents its entrance.

Jesus was home. He had arrived in Nazareth in the midst of being exposed to that part of the world as the miracle worker. He had already gained a reputation. Crowds gathered just to hear him speak; people gathered the sick and brought them to his feet. Religious intellectuals would confront him in the streets, questioning his methods of mending the societal breach, all which only increased his popularity. He was a champion of the poor and oppressed. He was a healer of the human heart and body. But when he arrived in his hometown, even though these things were known, he was not well received. Instead they asked, "Where does this man get this power?" or rather, "Who does Jesus think he is?" The question is valid. It is appropriate to ask and understand where one's faith is to be placed. They are asking the right question but there are limited possible answers. The source of the power is either good or bad. And the power is either natural or beyond nature. Simply, the validity and power of the words and works of Christ were either from heaven, or earth, or hell. Tragically, the answer of Jesus' neighbors was incorrect. The rest of Palestine had to understand his work, words, and validity without the benefit of knowing his history, and they accepted him. But here in his own hometown, where the people could assess and know that his words and work were consistent with his life, family, and history, they rejected him. Here, those who should've known him best, understood him least, blinded by the nearsightedness of their experience. So in Nazareth, where Christ returned to share heaven's gifts of hope and healing to the ones he had known all his human life, the miracle-worker was stymied.

As awesome as God is, and no matter how great God's desire to open heaven's gates to bless our lives, the Divine's opportunity to do so is limited by us. And we set the limits of our lives according to who we think Christ is. The question is the lock on a massive door, and our answer is the only key.

Martha said to Jesus . . . "Lord if you had been here,
my brother would not have died."
John 11:21

Caught in the apparent caprice of Christ, Martha does not seek compassion or the compliance necessary to accept the dark finality of fate but instead confronts the Creator of the Universe.

Together with her sister, Mary, and her brother, Lazarus, Martha had become a friend and follower of Jesus. The Gospel suggests that the nature of the relationship of this family and the Master was intimate, even though it remains unrecorded. Surely, Jesus had sat at their table and enjoyed their company. Perhaps together they had teased meaning from the tenor of their times and talked of God's glory in the midst of and despite the Roman presence in the sacred lands of Palestine.

Martha's heart must have felt the warm embrace of God's peace in those times. But now her heart and mind must have been twisted as she contrasted her reality with her hope. You cannot be betrayed whenever Jesus stopped by, but what of his absence and what now of his presence? She must have known and longed for the joy that permeated the place as the Master spoke of the mysteries and meaning of life. The light Jesus brought transcended space and time, and a love that illuminated God's active presence must have warmed her heart, but now tragedy abruptly entered her home and her hopes betrayed her. Lazarus had become ill. As the illness progressed and remedy failed, the chill of death loomed close. Some were sent to summon the Savior. The healing power of Jesus was needed to save the soul of Martha and heal the sick body of her brother. Martha loved her brother. Jesus tarried. Lazarus died. Martha retorts.

Hope never just hangs around like ripe fruit bending unattended branches, finally falling to the earth to fade into fruitlessness. Hope is like the brilliant lighting flash in the midst of starless black gloom momentarily illuminating the path through danger. Hope must be held tighter even as it fades from the flash before your eyes to the faint memory of your mind.

> *Mary said, "I am the Lord's servant! Let it happen as you have said." And the angel left her.*
> *Luke 1:38 (CEV)*

And the Lord sent the message to Mary, "I wish to occupy all of your intimate space."

The angel came to Mary with a unique and dangerous proclamation. The message, which causes concern and confusion in the heart and mind of the young Mary, is so august that it requires her continual assurance that the reason she was chosen for this assignment is because she is favored. The task she is being asked to perform is a private, intimate, and spiritual assent to the will of God for her personal life. Yet, this very holy deed will surely result in a public, obvious, and physical condemnation and shame. No assurance could have blinded Mary from a realization of the difficulty of the request. It is why she immediately asks the question that will haunt her in the eyes, minds, and mouths of all who see her obedience for the rest of her life. How did this happen? Whose child is this? The religious would surely scoff and many pious persons would berate and belittle Mary because her obedience to God would so resemble their disobedience to God. But Mary reminded herself and us that we are the servants of the Almighty and released her total self with all her holy parts to the incomprehensible and problematic prerogative of

God. We look at the mother of Jesus with eyes of awe and honor. We lift her faithfulness beyond all others and imagine ourselves free from opportunities to follow her footsteps. But we view the past through colored lenses, which obscure important facets of the jewel formed in the crucible of obedience. Mary yielded her most sacred space to God and became a mystery the world could not understand for more than thirty years. But God had chosen her above all the women of all time. Her consent brought her shame for thirty years . . . and glory forever.

The paradox of the kingdom paradigm is that we must give up our lives to gain them. Our suffering, in what may seem the everlasting present, is infinitesimally small and transient compared to the promised paradise and glory of the everlasting future. What God asked of Mary, God asks of us.

You have heard the blasphemy: What think ye?
And they all condemned him to be guilty of death.
Mark 14:64

When those who have left the rigor of faith for the trappings of religion hear the voice of truth or are exposed to the reality of God they cry blasphemy. Religions begin to limit God when they incarcerate the imagination of the people of God or chain the people to the past while seeking to subject them to submissive roles in the present beneath the "authorized" leaders. But God remains free to move and to speak to whomever and whenever God chooses and thereby will always confound the self-authorized and their confused understanding.

It is the trial of Jesus. And even in this unorthodox travesty of Jewish justice there is inconclusive evidence of Jesus' guilt. The high priest, elders, and the scribes have assembled in the darkness to cover their nefarious plan, the trial, and condemnation of Jesus. Their contrived trial included pre-selected adversaries of this Jesus. The stage was set. The players had their parts. Then the travesty began as they brought the bound and already condemned Master into the theater of the profane. But even the nefarious can be affected by light, as the priests are unable to condemn Jesus, even with the contrived testimony against him. Throughout the court cacophony, Jesus remained silent. Whether beneath his controlled demeanor there raged a tempest or calm we cannot know, but as the bribed and the bitter paraded their lies and witless witnesses against him, Christ spoke no word. The high priest, perhaps embarrassed by the inability of the drama to demand the desired condemnation of Christ, takes matters into his own hands and addresses the Master himself: "Are you the Savior our fathers said would come?" Are you the Son of God in ways no one else has ever been or could ever be? It was a question that silence could not answer. Jesus spoke an emphatic "I am" and added a sobering prophetic truth, "Soon you shall see me sitting at God's right hand and returning to take over the world." The statement was all the rulers needed. Christ was condemned and sent to the cross.

The one man that the rulers despised and rejected was the one sent to save them. Christ could save them from the Romans but he could not save them from themselves, and so determined never to bow down before Christ they died in their depravity complicit in the unjust and illegal condemnation of their only hope.

So the people sent to Shiloh, that they might bring the ark
of the covenant of the Lord from there . . .
1 Samuel 4:4

God is no good luck charm. God is no portable, manipulatable power awaiting our disposition.

The children of Israel amassed themselves on the battlefield pitched against their nemesis, the Philistines. They knew themselves to be the chosen of God, the direct descendants of those for whom the Divine slew the Egyptians. They thought their God was of absolute power, beyond the power of the gods whom the other nations worshipped. They knew that the God of Abraham and Sarah, Isaac and Rebecca, Jacob and Leah was the God who would deliver. This is the God who overthrew mighty kingdoms and controlled the very forces of nature on behalf of their ancestors. This is the God who, with Moses, defeated kingdoms both great and small. And these children of Israel not only knew that God delivered, they believed they knew the mechanism God provided to effect that deliverance, the Ark. Their history declared it, their rituals celebrated it, their hearts assumed it, and their minds fashioned a plan to launch the divine secret weapon against their enemies. They believed they possessed the military hardware of the Almighty, while unaware that the Divine was not in possession of their hearts. And with a confidence emboldened by ignorance they brought what was holy into their manipulative plan, and with a triumphant shout they crossed the battlefield to engage their enemy. But their charm failed and the Philistines put them to flight. Four thousand of Israel's men were slain and their army withdrew in defeat.

To assume is to refuse to examine the explained. In the mundane machinations of our material lives, assumptions are understandable, forgivable, and often correctable. But to refuse to examine our own current explanations of God is to diminish the nature of an autonomous God and invite disaster. To project the course of current events into the future or to seek to replay the past in the present is a cry for annihilation. Often this cry is driven by the very ones who regard themselves as the inheritors of divine grace and the arbiters of Christ's presence in the world. But if humanity is to wrest catastrophe from the jaws of destiny our current path must be altered. We must examine ourselves and our motives in ways that expose our assumptions as good luck charms and invite the independent intervention of an Almighty and autonomous God.

Remember me Oh Lord with the favor with which you
have shown to thy people. Oh visit me with thy salvation.
Psalm 106:4

Human life is distinguished from the beasts of nature most by its capacity, propensity, and ability to be stifled by the anxiety created by our own momentarily imagined reality. The propensity to be unsatisfied and to desire most what we lack, resides in the heart of both the pauper and the prince. The ability to excel, motivated by these desires, defines the greatest of human example. The capacity to be depressed and feel diminished by their absence is a singularly defining flaw of the human creation. Yet it is this desire for fulfillment, embodied in and emboldened by the actions of our daily lives, which is the witness of our utter need for God.

We are not given the particular details of the Psalmist's anxiety in this text, but the forty-seventh verse suggests that the difficulties may reside in the concept of the "abject other." Being the stranger in a strange land and subject to the villainy and vulgarity of alien status is a life pressure, that transcends class or vocation. Whether this is the case or not, the focus in the psalm is not the psalmist's pain. Most of this psalm's forty-eight verses recount the faithfulness of God in contrast to the unfaithfulness of the people of the past. Its central point is that problems do not descend indiscriminately or recklessly into our lives. They do not combine to create the chaos into which our lives are so often invited, but our problems are products of a Divine plan in which we are complicit and God is active. The remedy therefore is to be reminded of God's provision and mercy. Such a mind is prepared by the expectation of God's plan, provision and providence ultimately ruling in life.

A problem is a situation or circumstance, that is not equal to our expectation and preparation. When we find ourselves stressed and anxious in a situation, it is an indication of our unpreparedness and of our inability to realize God's providence, provision and ability.

From the rising of the sun even unto the going down of
the same my name shall be great among the Gentiles . . .
Malachi 1:11

God does not wait for the praises of people. The Divine does not depend on the dances of men and is independent of the sacrifice of those who count themselves in divine service. The mountains rise to great height in worship, the oceanic bottoms bow low in humble praise. And the strangers of the earth whisper sweetly God's name in delight of the Divine presence.

Malachi writes years after the Jews, who had been dispersed throughout the known world, returned to Jerusalem. Exiled, many recanted the unfaithfulness of their fore parents and renewed their commitment to the covenant of Moses. Embarking on the pilgrimage of piety, they left the comforts of Babylon and returned to their home and heritage. Upon their return, great feasts of piety and greater promises of faithfulness were made before the repaired altar of the Lord. They had restored the temple, but it was a shadow of its former glory. The priests had been appointed and anointed for their service. But now, the fervor and integrity of the revival, once led by Ezra and Nehemiah, had waned. The priests labored at the altar of sacrifice, but leering lethargy led them toward loathing the Levitical service and their obligations. Corruptions in the sanctified process arose anew and the priests grew tired of their obligations. Upon such a sea, Malachi proclaims that God is independent of their obedience. God is not insulted by their self-exalting vanity, but rather the priests are diminished by the blindness born of their irreverence. This is because the sacrifices of praise and obedience ascend like incense to the throne of God from those who the priests count as alien to God.

The outsider is on the inside because the gatekeepers are unaware of the entrance God has opened to the nations. The heavens declare the glory and the earth resounds God's praise in perpetuity. To be silent is to be lost. To be vain in one's oblations is to flee into the empty refuge of cold and barren space.

Be careful for nothing; but in everything by prayer and
supplication with thanksgiving let your requests be made
known to God.
Philippians 4:6

There is no known beast in the kingdom of the wild that worries about tomorrow. The squirrel, which scurries to hide nuts in places he will forget, does not worry. The lion, fierce and fast, does not fret about the failing herds or the fading forests. The eagle, who exchanges her mountain perch for the penthouse by the park, does not pine away in the dark lamenting lost yesterdays. Alone, the beings that imagine themselves intelligent loose their overpowered yet underutilized minds in the menagerie of fantasized memories and the montage of fright-filled projections of their present and future.

Paul and Timothy write to the people of the church in Philippi who are laboring to enter into the rest of God. The process of becoming Christians and the progress of their faith has caused anxiety in the community. The Apostles exhort the church with the examples of themselves and Christ to encourage its spiritual growth. Yet, both writer and reader understand the tension produced by living as a Christian in an unchristian world. Somehow, neither the accepted truth of the Gospel nor the victory and power of Christ has delivered them from the melancholy of the mundane or the manic excesses of the material. So the Apostles rehearse the salvation history of the community and their own testimonies. Timothy has proven he is a servant of the gospel; Epaphroditus worked for Christ until he was in ill health and near death; Paul, with his impeccable background, pressed forward in hope; and even Christ himself became a slave to fulfill the will of the Father. We are all subject to the chaos and confusion of the unregenerate world. Tomorrow is always the "known" unknown. Today is always dominated by our control of our dark thoughts. But we are to rejoice, not oblivious to the struggles within and between us but impervious to their eternal consequence.

Give thanks because God is in charge and you can ask God to move on your behalf. There is nothing in our imagined yesterday or our experience of today or our projections of tomorrow that can remove us from God.

Then Satan answered the Lord and said,
"Does Job fear God for nothing?"

Job 1:9

The true believer should have no reason at all for believing in God. Our trust and faith in the Almighty must at the most critical times of our lives exist independent of chaotic or contrary circumstances. If we believe in God because things are good or because we think God wants our life and the things around us to be good, our faith is not trust in God . . . it is hope in a good luck charm.

On one sunny day in the realm of the Divine, Satan saunters up before the throne of Almighty God. God takes the opportunity to display one of heaven's treasures and asks Satan "have you considered my servant Job . . ." Satan retorts to the challenge with the charge that God has protected Job with a hedge. He asserts that God's blessings were the cause of Job's prosperity and too many believe the devil's word on the cause of Job's reality. But, Satan is the false accuser; it is his task to maliciously malign the character or reputation of another. And here Satan is impugning the character of God with his charge that God provided Job with prosperity, and that this prosperity was the source of his piety. Yet there is no reason we should believe the words of Satan against the person of God. Job's prosperity was not a result of God's hedge and his piety was not a product of his prosperity. The book of Job is God's witness to Job and us that Job's love and devotion to God were independent of his physical or material condition. Job served God for nothing. In fact, when Job's life was stripped of all he cared for, he, through his barely pious prayers, provoked a revelation of God's person that increased and completed his faith.

If we are true believers, we believe in God as an act of our will without regard to the heaven or hell of our lives. In fact, when we believe in God through the horrors of our lives it is only then that we can be sure we are indeed God's.

. . . and it was told Saul that David was escaped from Keilah:
and he forebear to go forth.
1 Samuel 23:13

The past is not always clear. You cannot always know if you did the right thing or followed faithfully by looking back. Following God involves an ongoing decision-making process whereby one must discern the will of God for oneself in the present instant. Later reflection on that time and decision will not always reveal the godliness or appropriateness of the decision.

David was a fugitive hiding in the wilderness and all the disenfranchised of Israel gathered themselves to him. David had the task of developing those who joined him into a formidable force. He had to transform them from a crowd of disaffected misfits into a well-tuned and goal-oriented community. And he had to do this while eluding the pursuit of his sworn enemy. Saul and his army of hired mercenaries were continually on David's trail. David and his group had delivered the city of Keilah and were living there instead of in the wilderness. It was rumored that Saul was headed to Keilah, and David's men wanted to stay in the city behind its protecting walls. Then David, rather than simply heeding the wisdom of those he led, asked the Lord for guidance. The Lord told David that the citizens of Keilah would betray him, so David and his six hundred men left and headed for the hills. When Saul heard that David left Keilah, he turned around and never saw the walled city. Reflecting back on leaving the city, David and his men might have wondered if the rumor of Saul's nearness and intent were true or if the citizens of Keilah would have actually betrayed them.

Looking back on the warmth and security of Keilah from the cold and barren wilderness revealed no obvious evidence that it was wise to leave. You cannot, by looking backward, always authenticate the will or work of God in your life. Often only God knows the daisy chain of destructive events our disobedience would cause. We must be able to discern the will of God and walk in it without the confirmation of collateral circumstance.

So they read in the book of the law of God distinctly,
and gave the sense, and caused them to understand the reading.
Nehemiah 8:8

Many good Bible readers are too confident in what they believe to be the truth of God. Doctors study medicine in great schools and for extended periods and gain great deference. Lawyers go to school and command great respect. Psychologists apply honed skills of observation and are nearly worshipped as gods. But the trained minister's notion of God's requirement is often utterly dispensable, and that most often in the very church they serve.

Nehemiah and Ezra, after they had been blessed by God in the restorative work in Jerusalem, and after they had led the people in the rebuilding of the wall and city gates, call a solemn assembly of the children of Israel. The emigrants of Babylon, who had returned to the homeland of their fore parents, had little understanding of the God of Abraham. They had heard of Moses and the law and they understood themselves to be distinct from others but had no intimate knowledge of the will of God for their daily lives. Ezra and Nehemiah erected a podium and gathered the people around them to hear the reading of the word of God. It was read in the ancient tongue of their fore parents, interpreted, and explained. The meaning and message break the heart of those who now understand. But the reason the people were convicted is because Nehemiah and Ezra had already been convicted through careful prayer and study of God's word. These two had applied themselves to the word of God and the word of God to themselves and had been changed by the process. Now they were able to instruct others.

We should not be cavalier regarding the presentation of the word of God. We must study to show ourselves approved unto God and recognize and require those who are anointed to present God's truth to study even more. Good Christians would not think to perform surgery or prescribe medications without the proper preparation. Faithful saints would cower before a full courtroom and likewise we should approach the throne of God with awe, reverence, and reticence and do his servants no harm.

*Create in me a clean heart oh God . . . Cast me not away
from thy presence; and take not thy Holy Spirit from me.
Restore to me the joy of thy salvation and uphold me.*
Psalms 51:11-12

When I am convinced and convicted of sin and unable to find hope in self-righteousness, I wonder just where I am in the kingdom of God. There are times when I weary of working for God and long for God to make me aware of Divine cleansing and hope. In the shrill of cold abandonment, I hope that I may feel the fires of salvation as the joy of the Lord washes over my soul.

David sat high above the rebuke of his servants. He is mature now, having fought through the ignorant arrogance of adolescence and the valiant virility of young adulthood, and has become king. His lust for the Lord, ignited to hot flame in righteous rebellion of the rejected of God and heated hopes of Heaven's help, has left him and been replaced by confidence in God's completed call. Bereft of the pain of becoming, he sits in the seat of one who has arrived at a long awaited station and calls it his throne. There he sat, satisfied and self-sanctified, until the servant of God appeared, pointing the finger of God at the hole in the king's garment. David acting as a king had taken and discarded with impunity. Now, the spirit of God, through the voice of the prophet, points out the open and festering wound David's acts have caused in his own soul. But David is blessed because he was not left in the ignorance of his own actions or the arrogance of his office. The rebuke woke in him the longing to be holy and provoked in him the cry for help.

As children of the New Testament, we are to be confident of God's grace and heaven's unmerited favor. We are to walk as Christians fully aware of the freedom bought by Calvary's sacrifice but recognize that this same freedom may lead us to hell. We live in this tension; never so confidant as to take grace for granted and never fully fearing the hell, which beckons us. To be human is to fail and fall short, but to be satisfied is to extinguish the very fire of your soul.

*For the Son of man is come to seek and to save
that which was lost.
Luke 19:10*

There is no greater joy than to be rescued. There is no greater horror
than the revelation that you are lost. The child who wanders away from his
parent is often initially playful and happy. Called away from the safety of a
parent's side by curiosity or mischief, the child roams oblivious to his predicament. Drawn away from the proper course by the dubious or the evil, the
child enjoys the first fresh moments of freedom. Then the horror hits with the
realization that he is alone. Then a sadness that rises from his soul is shown
on his face and heard in the alarm sounded by his voice.

The story of Zaccheus is set against the story of the rich young ruler
in the preceding chapter. Both men have obstacles between them and Jesus.
Both have become prosperous by wandering away from God in pursuit of
that which can never fully satisfy. But both are aware of the hole in their souls
and seek Jesus. The ruler meets the Lord and leaves in sorrow. Zaccheus
fellowships with the Lord and finds joy. Love to one is stark and demanding,
to the other warm and inviting. The ruler is sent to ruin the riches that were
his identity. But the hunger of Zaccheus's soul is satisfied by the acceptance
of Jesus, who sat at his table, and he is changed forever. Jesus did not have to

instruct him. Zaccheaus knew what to do because he was no longer lost but partnered again with the God of every heart's deepest desire.

The greatest blessing riches can give is the wisdom that riches are insufficient to meet the needs of one's soul. In fact, the greatest blessing life can offer is the revelation that we are not where we wish to be and utterly unable to find our way. You can only fully experience the joy of the Lord when you fully experience the depths of your depravity. Soon after we are born we all begin to wander away from God, until either because of the snares of the devil or the desires of our own little lusts we are lost. But the blessing of being lost is waking to the desire to be found and the dearest name of our Lord, is Savior.

The people answered and said, Thou hast a devil . . .
John 7:20

There are times when I think I must be an ass and a fool. There are those who seek to convince me that the demons I see must be reflections of me. My life has been littered with the harm that comes with living. I have learned not to languish over the pain or problems of human existence. I have suffered no less than others and perhaps no more, but when those who have inflicted pain upon my soul and those who have charred me black with the fire of their wrath and hatred look deep into my eyes and induce the insanity that identifies me as the sole persecutor of my oft beleaguered soul, I am left of my right mind and believe myself the demon.

The religious men around Jesus had grown tired of his condemnation of their injustice and indictment of their hypocrisy. The popularity of Jesus was waning, yet Jesus, as if oblivious to the danger, teaches in the temple. A deal had been struck with the devil and Judas had already agreed to betray the Master. The religious leaders confront him, questioning his credentials and his doctrine. Jesus responds in defense of his teaching and certifies his knowledge of their plot to kill him. But instead of repenting or even retiring to some dark corner, the conspirators attack the Way, the Truth, and the Life and accuse him of being demon possessed.

It is human nature not to see one's fault, but there are those who would not see their wrong if Jesus showed it to them. These invite the spirit of Satan into themselves and remain ready to accuse others. Beware of allowing such to enter or remain in your sphere of influence for the self-justifying circle of their thoughts will ultimately seek to convince you that you are mad.

And if the house be worthy, let your peace come upon it,
but if it is not worthy let your peace return unto you.
Matthew 10:13

It is unusual to ask for someone to return a gift you have given them, whether they are making good use of the gift or not. But there are some gifts that you must take back.

Jesus was moved by his love for the multitude, so he called the twelve disciples to his side. He charged them and gave them power to cast out unclean spirits and heal all kinds of diseases. He sent them out to preach the gospel of the Kingdom of heaven to the lost sheep of the house of Israel with specific instructions. The disciples were to take no provisions for themselves but rather should rely on the good will and kindness of the people whom they met. They were to enter a town or village and inquire as to which home would be the most welcoming and worthy and there abide. However, Jesus tells them, there may be homes into which they are invited that would be unworthy of the spirit that they would bring, homes with compassion but no peace. In such homes, Jesus understood that the disciples might lose their peace by adopting the problem paradigm of the home. Instead, the disciples would have to choose to not get caught up in the unworthy thoughts and experiences of their hosts and redeem their peace.

Peace is the product of harmony. One has peace emanating from his or her soul when they are secure in the love of God and the knowledge that they are actively doing God's will. Peace radiates from a person as warm rays emanate from the sun, and when that peace is confronted with confusion, anger, or unrest it seeks to return to the soul from which it came. When you offer the gift of friendship and it is misused and unappreciated you should let it come back or you would not be a friend to yourself. When you offer the gift of love and it is belittled or destroyed, let it come back, before you begin to think yourself unworthy of being loved. Enjoin and enjoy the peace God gives you whether those around you have peace or not.

And David said in his heart, I shall now perish one day by
the hand of Saul . . .
1 Samuel 27:1

Stress is the energy upon which life exists. The tension produced by the
difference between what is and what is wished to be is the energy that propels
the engine of our existence. It is human nature to long for what is lacked
and depreciate what is gained. Humanity serves both itself and God when it
appreciates the torture born of its sense of incompleteness.

The little boy David, dissatisfied with the obligations of a shepherd,
marches into the goliath of conflict and becomes a soldier. Unsatisfied with
singing the praises of the king, he encourages the young women to sing of
him and incurs the suspicions of Saul. Unable to act suitably subservient or
submissive, the decorated soldier deserts his duties. Although anointed and
appointed heir to God's people, he inherits the malcontents in the wilderness
and the misfits on the plain. Then after years of flight as a fugitive, David
openly defies the king. Twice he had been afforded the opportunity to slay the
seeker of his soul. Twice he stood able to end his life as a fugitive by ending
the life of his enemy. But constrained by obedience to the God of the paradox
he preserved the life of the one desiring to take his life. Then when David
reveals to the army of Saul his restraint, Saul repents. When Saul repents,

David finally believes with his whole heart that he will die by the hand of Saul. So in fear David flees to the Philistines, and trapped between these two enemies he tiptoes his way along the path God had ordained for him.

We live in such a way as to produce and increase the tensions around us in order that God would ultimately appear and bring the peace we are so utterly incomplete without. And so we are never satisfied with all we have until all we have is God. The moments of our greatest peace are when all hope has either failed or been abandoned except the ludicrous hope in God.

Why stand ye gazing up into heaven?
Acts 1:11

The substance of the gospel and the energy of the believer's faith must be expended to and through the people he or she encounters if faith in Jesus is to be genuine. Anything less is an endorsement of hell's claim on our world.

The disciples of Jesus had just been through three horrific heart-rending days and nights. Just prior to the nightmare, they had walked and talked with the master as his closest earthly companions. They were the believing elite privy to the evening reflections and morning prayers of the Master. For three years they gleaned the harvest of heaven, hearing and holding every word of the Master, then the night came. Then Jesus was betrayed by a brother, convicted in a kangaroo court, and crucified. They all ran in hurt and horror each to their own way. But when their hope was all but gone the women brought good news of the resurrection and in time they each saw, heard, and touched their Savior. Jesus gathers them and gives his final instructions, then rises through the air to assume his place in heaven. The disciples stand transfixed with eyes on the sky as if their gaze could carry their souls behind their beloved Savior. But the message from God, sent through the angel, was to get their minds and bodies centered on God's purpose for them in the earth and off their hopes in heaven. The Lord's work on earth was done but their work had just begun. While they focused on heaven they could not see the need for Christ working through them on the earth. Their focus on heaven fought Jesus' last command and the meaning of his walk on earth. For a moment they forgot the Lord's plan and their purpose. Our sights must be fixed on fulfilling the work of Christ in the earth to have any real hope of heaven.

Heaven's Christ is not beyond us to be longed for but among us to be realized. Now communion with our Lord is found in our worship and in the experience of community.

Let the day perish wherein I was born, and the night in which it
was said, there is a man-child conceived. Let that day be darkness;
let not God regard it from above, neither let the light Shine upon it.
Job 3:3-4

Depression is a bear trap snapped onto the heart, compelling the muscle to contract and never expand again. It is a disease, which colors all of life in a darkened hue. Such sorrow may be triggered by calamity's crash into our sublime imagination of life or it may result from our own chemical biology sabotaging our very being. But when sorrow arrives it begins to sink the soul, no matter what source first punctured life's buoyancy.

Job lost more than any other Old Testament character we know. Before his terror, Job lived a righteous and prosperous life. His religion was devout, his relationship with God praiseworthy. He was very rich, having hundreds of herds with thousands of cattle, servants, fields, family, and good friends. In fact, Job was such an example of godliness that the Almighty suggested Job to the Devil, the enemy of our souls, as an example of a divine servant. Satan in response suggests affliction would cause Job to curse God. He asks for and receives permission to put the demonic notion to the test. The destroyer descends upon Job's life and in one day causes Job to lose all his wealth, including his children, who are attacked and slain. But as the news of catastrophe cascades over his broken heart, Job falls to his face and worships God. Unsuccessful and unsatisfied, Satan requests permission for bodily affliction and when granted causes boils to break out from the soles of Job's feet to the crown of his head. These tragedies moved Job from the enviable place of pleasure and prosperity to the realm of the despised and rejected of men. It was more than Job thought he could bear. Friends assembled to comfort him and together they sat in silence for seven days. Only then after unthinkable travesty, aided by the contemplations of a broken heart, was the despair complete and Job cursed the day he was born.

No one depression is more righteous than another. No one sorrow more salient than the next. Each of us enters the darkness from our own path. Yet our sorrow itself reveals that there is a force inside us, which desperately desires life. When it is hard to imagine life, love, and hope beyond the present horror we must believe recklessly that God loves us particularly. Love alone rules in the realm of sorrow; reason here is reduced to the ridiculous.

And when ye spread forth your hands, I will hide mine
eyes from you: yea, when ye make many prayers,
I will not hear: your hands are full of blood.
Isaiah 1:15

We who are clearly seen cannot see. God is independent. God is neither a reflection of our noblest thoughts nor a projection of our best selves. We create through our actions and in our worship idols that are mere circus mirror images of our minor selves, and we bow low before this reflection we call God. But God is God's own construction.

The prophet Isaiah speaks in solemn voice to a nation preoccupied with her own presence and to a people who presume too much about themselves and their relationship with the Almighty. The world of Isaiah was in flux. The Assyrian ascendance to hegemony had yet to affect the tiny nation. Jerusalem was a complex and cosmopolitan city, comfortable in her ignorance. Within her gates the strands of her economy, society, and theology wove an intricate fabric. She was a city whose system centered on her highest hill and temple. She was a stratified hive of the rich, the not rich, and the poor with a devout belief in her particularity among the people and places in the world. She was the city, and within her were the people of the Almighty God. But constructing an acceptable notion of the divine is not synonymous with being accepted by the Divine. And as the people worshipped in the sanctuary of God, believing themselves to be offering the highest praise to the God who has chosen them, Isaiah is allowed to peer through divine lenses to behold the scene, and what he sees is repulsive. The celebrants engaged in what they believe to be wonderful worship cannot see that they are covered in the blood and shame of willful arrogance against and ignorance of the very God they propose to celebrate.

We remain blind to the utter depravity capable within the human heart until accosted by the inconceivable and horrid act of another. But the hardened heart and corrupted mind, which reside and grow hidden in the demented darkness of a soul, is always in open light before God. We are left only one weapon against our own proclivity, to approach the presence of the Almighty in full knowledge of our ignorance. We only come before God undone and unclean in desperate search of a grace we cannot deserve.

For if thou altogether "hold your peace at this time . . ."
Esther 4:14

Our choices determine who we will become, not what will happen. Too often I have heard the lament of someone who has done their best to succeed but failed, or tried their hardest to avoid harm but found themselves in utter heartbreak and horror. In such circumstances the cry "if only I . . ." emanates through the tears and pain. But the assumption that individual action can preclude or prevent the proclivities of life obfuscates the Providence of God.

Esther had paid any debt she owed Mordecai. He had raised his orphaned cousin as his own and presented her in the beauty pageants for the King until she sat as queen. She had followed his instructions, forfeiting independence of mind, even marriage, and given her body, if not soul, to the King. Further, her new position provided Mordecai access to the King, so she had honored her cousin and could live the rest of her life in ignominy, sheltered, and protected with the rest of the King's objects. But the lives of the Jews of Persia were threatened with extinction. Those who had seen and survived the blood and death of their parents, children, and loved ones in the diaspora found themselves again under the light of suspicion held in the dark hands of death. Mordecai marches in sackcloth and ashes to the ear of Esther and presents her with his final proposition. She is to go to the King and plead for the lives of her people. She responds with questions that underscore the danger of approaching the King, and then her cousin declares that even if she doesn't say a word the Jews will be delivered. Esther asks for a covering of prayer and then chooses to risk her life to save her people.

Esther participated with Providence and won a place in the admiration of her people and the canon. Esther's obedience may have been superfluous to the deliverance of the Jews but it was essential to the deliverance of Esther.

And when Saul inquired of the Lord, the Lord answered
him not, not by dreams, nor Urim, nor prophets . . .
1 Samuel 28:6

There is a place of darkness into which no light can shine. There is a coldness of soul no fire can warm. It is the human heart that God has vacated. It is the soul whose prayers cannot reach the ear of the Divine. It is the end of a long misdirected walk through life.

Saul sees the host of the Philistines and is afraid. The fears he spent his life avoiding have completed the corruption of his heart, and the would-be king cowers. Worthless to God and hopeless in himself, he pines away in desperate despair. The years of God's deliverance have taught him nothing about battle, his unrequited quest to murder David have taught him nothing about the futility of insolence, and so he falls to the earth prayerfully with no God to hear him. He seeks help tearfully with no God to see him. He fasts but his heart is not open to find faith. He is lost in his own land, alone in the midst of his own people, condemned by his dead conscious, and in this region of the damned he still cannot repent. He finds no redemption in all his sorrow because his sorrow is self-centered and self-serving. His prayers preclude Providence because they are empty of all but fear and regret. So God, too just to comfort him, too wise to console him, and too righteous to conform to his marred image of divinity, leaves Saul alone. Saul unable to trust his life in the care of the Lord, whom he had not come to know, languishes for lament and uses the name of the Lord to swear at the feet of a witch. Saul in self-induced insanity decides to seek the service of the sorceress and seals his soul in the service of Satan.

We have the ability to encourage the insanity of our own soul. We have the right to choose bareness and despair. We can choose to become bereft of God, cold and alone, and die in hopelessness pining away an empty eternity. We need only to walk through life with each silent step centered on ourselves; we need only to long for the praises of people; we need only never to repent.

Then I was very very afraid, and said to the king . . .
why should not my countenance be sad . . .
Nehemiah 2:2-3

Prayer should not be a postcard addressed to "whom it May concern" anywhere in heaven. Prayer should not be our request, sealed in the bottle of hope, cast and forgotten into the sea of our circumstances. Prayer is a plea before the eternal and almighty seat of power. Prayer is the opportunity to collaborate and cooperate with the one who controls the cosmos. But for prayer to be effective it must be central to our concerns and emanate from the center of our being. It must be a lifeline we grasp on this side of reality that tethers us to the eternal.

Nehemiah was in anguish because of the state of those who dwelt in Jerusalem. The city had become a scarred shadow of its former glory, and the people lived in peril and poverty. Nehemiah heard the cry from deep within him for the restoration of the city of peace. So the cupbearer began to pray. He prayed privately confessing the sins of the nation and those of his own heart. For four months, he prayed, fasted, and afflicted his soul on behalf of Jerusalem and her people until the Lord heard his plea and began to answer. But the sorrow of Nehemiah's prayers began to show on his face, and when Nehemiah attended to his duties in the presence of the King his prayers betrayed him. To frown in front of a king could cost you your life. Nehemiah's private prayers were displayed in public on his frame and face. When the King inquired about his insolence, instead of repenting he was emboldened and made his case for his beleaguered brothers.

Fervent prayer emboldens you beyond the preoccupation of your own predicament and brings you before the throne of God on behalf of those in desperate need. Fervent prayer makes you bold before your enemies, ready for adversity, and more aware of God than your surroundings. Prayer may put you in peril of your life so that you may witness the power of God commissioned by your contrition.

This is the day the Lord has made;
I will rejoice and be glad in it.
Psalm 118:24

Entropy is never overcome by thought. To overcome the regressive force of the cursed earth requires focus and vigilance. As this whirling planet careens through the cosmos, disorder increases. Exploited by the rich, ignored by the masses, and fought off by the few, entropy seeks to wear away our hopes and empty our souls. To rejoice is an act of our volition against the river of wanton worry and fret. To stand up is to fight gravity and to be glad is to defy the laws of thermodynamics. We decide to be glad like we decide to exercise. We decide to rejoice like we decide to brush our teeth. To fail to do so is to stand as castles of sand against the rising tide.

The Psalmist calls out to the Lord from his distress. The forces of his enemies, like swarming bees, are arrayed against him, and he is out numbered. They have hit him hard in hopes of knocking him down in defeat. His wounds invite death to his side but his trust is in the Lord, and he commands death to depart. Even when the Lord chastens him, he trusts in this same Lord for help. His cry, "this is the day that the Lord has made," declares the ultimate force of his life and the universe. His decision to "rejoice and be glad in it" is the commitment that declares God to be Lord in the whole of his life. When the chief priests and elders of the people of Israel question the validity and authority of Jesus' ministry, words, and work, Jesus returns to the power of this Psalm to stand up against the gravity of their attack. They sought to diminish him by rejection, and he took refuge in the choice to rejoice in the face of rebuke.

This world condones worry, encourages the wicked in their pernicious ways, and works to tear down what is built up. We choose either to "rejoice and be glad" or are defeated in the hope of life. God will not override our choice or always encourage it; nevertheless, when we choose to rejoice it is God alone who imbues that choice with the power that raises our spirits and reverses our demise.

But he was on his way to Jerusalem, so the people there
refused to welcome him.
Luke 9:53 (CEV)

When you learn of or experience someone's hatred of you, you have only two choices: you can choose to love them or you can choose to hate yourself. You can seek to lift the other into a light that will reflect to them the God that is in them or you can plunge yourself into a self deprecating darkness that will blind you to your own salvation and seek to validate the very hatred with which you were harmed.

Jesus was nearing the end of his mission on the earth. While on his way to Jerusalem, he instructed some of his followers to go into Samaria and acquire a place suitable for their needs. The Samaritans, however, aware of and angered by the fact that Jesus was on his way to Jerusalem, refused to let him stay in their town. When the disciples heard report of this rejection, they asked if they could call down fiery retribution for the rejection. But Jesus understood that both rejections were wrong. The Samaritans rejected Jesus because he seemed to accept the Jews. The Samaritans had been ridiculed and hated by their southern relatives, who identified themselves as full-blooded descendants of Abraham, Isaac, and Jacob. The animosity of the two groups grew as they clung to competitive myths of ethnicity. But the Samaritan's rejection of Jesus did not adversely affect the southern Jews, it hurt them. The disciples hoped to bring destructive retribution to those who had rejected them and their instructor, but they, too, were wrong. The hurt the disciples felt was made incendiary by the excessive power they believed they accessed, but power is not indicative of righteousness, and destruction does nothing to glorify a creator.

The disciples thought to defend Jesus by destroying those who had rejected him. But Jesus is not established by acceptance and is not threatened by rejection. The Samaritan village elders rejected Jesus and any help or hope that would accompany the Master's presence because Jesus seemed to accept Jews who rejected the Samaritans. But to reject Jesus is to expel yourself from eternal hope. To do so in the name of hurting your enemies is a demonic insanity.

If by any means I might attain unto the resurrection of the dead.
Not as though I had already attained . . .
Philippians 3:11

Heaven is an upward climb. The degradation of the saved soul comes not by the rebuke, scorn, or frown of others but as a result of entropy. It is natural for the foundations of our reality to erode. To enter into the Kingdom of God is to actively, intentionally, and continually witness the saving work of Christ in your life. The reason you must share the message of salvation is that in sharing, the good news of God is renewed within your soul. To be silent is to encourage doubt and fear. To remain in the company of those with whom you cannot actively share and demonstrate your faith is to invite cynicism and critique to the very foundation of your spiritual being.

The Apostle Paul had turned his life around. He enters the story of the early church as a religious zealot persecuting Christians. The resurrected Christ confronts him, and he is willingly converted and commissioned into Christian service. Paul then began a life committed to spreading the gospel and obeying the commands of Christ. Whereupon he was persecuted, rejected, stoned, and left for dead. He was cast in prison after being falsely accused and beaten by prison guards. God worked special miracles through him, and people were healed from the cloth that touched his body. All this occurred while he was diligently starting churches, preaching to the Gentiles, and discipling men and women in the work of the church. In fact, following Paul's conversion to Christ, there is no account of him backsliding, arguing, or disagreeing with the will of God for him. Yet, in the midst of such a life of service, Paul declares that he is neither overly confident nor complacent regarding the eternal salvation of his soul.

While we must not throwaway our confidence in Christ's ability to secure us in God, we must work as if our soul's salvation where dependent on our actions. To do otherwise is to allow lethargy to give birth to licentiousness.

But the spirit of the Lord departed from Saul and an evil spirit from the Lord troubled him.
1 Samuel 16:14

How can God send evil and not have evil as a part of the Divine nature? If it is God who sends evil to us, then are we not free from responsibility for the evil done under its influence? Such questions are encouraged by the passage above and suggest that the omniscience and omnipotence of God reduces humanity to puppets on a stage. But our inability to understand the particular acts of God should not preclude us from accepting the principles, which God unalterably operates. For God to remain just and loving we need only to lower our opinion of ourselves.

Saul had been handpicked by God to rule the tribal confederacy of Israel. Yet by the time of our scripture, Saul had disrespected God's prophet, offered an unholy sacrifice, cursed his son (and would have murdered him if not stopped by the people), caused the people to eat raw and bloody meat, and failed to obey God's battle instructions, all this without any help from an evil spirit. Further, our text does not say that God took the spirit of the Lord away from Saul but merely that God replaced that spirit with one more suited to Saul's frame.

There are spiritual and eternal consequences to our natural acts. To blame God for the divine responses is to attempt to justify our disobedience. The fact of all humanity working within the plan and prerogative of God does not preclude the independence of our personal choices. We will do God's will; our choice is whether we perform on God's stage as saints or devils.

*If we don't stop him now . . . everyone will put their faith
in him. Then the Romans will come and destroy
our temple and our nation.*
John 11:48 (CEV)

To invest in the security offered by the state is to forsake one's hope to caprice. To do so as an agent of God is the ultimate blasphemy.

It is the last days in the ministry of Jesus. His reputation has taken the small region of Palestine. People flock to him. Crowds search for him and follow him all day long, forsaking their normal investment and involvement with the world. But the religious rulers of the region were troubled. They understood their life's task to be the preservation of civil order in celebration and extension of their history—a history that held hopes for future deliverance from all oppression. But this Jesus movement was troubling, in part because it was beyond their ability to control and to conceive. The time caught them unprepared to accept that the God of their fathers would actually deliver them or that the Almighty would do so without their counsel and in a manner void of their approval. To further agitate the delicate balance of their position and the Roman rule of the region, this Jesus was raising people from the dead. This level of miraculous power was unprecedented except by the highest held prophets of their religious history. Yet, this Jesus had raised back to life several of the dead, and now he had raised Lazarus out of the grave after four days. Now, in addition to the activities of healings and teachings, they must contend for the hearts and religious minds of the people with someone who can raise the dead. The need to maintain their privileged positions blinded them to any possible personal benefit from the work or person of Jesus, so they determined to destroy him.

The religious rulers understood that the presence of Jesus, as well as the proliferation of his ethos, would be experienced by the Roman government as a threat to the social order. They believed that the Roman response to such a threat would be disastrous destruction of both symbol and substance of their leadership. So they decide to destroy the one who is manifesting the Almighty's miracle power in their midst to stave off their demotion and any destruction of the civil order. But in so doing they destroyed their only hope of realizing the true redemption of their historical hopes and any release from tyrannical Roman rule.

*I have heard of you by the hearing of the ear: but now see
you with my own eyes.*
Job 42:5

There are no benign encounters with God. To be confronted with the
presence, power, and person of God is to at once become aware of the utter
penury and lack of your humanity.

Job's trouble brought him face to face with God. The end of the travesty
in which Job was immersed by the divine into grave and unimaginable
horror afforded him the opportunity to see God and understand himself.
The God who invited the foul and evil Satan to destroy, test, and tempt
the property, person, and heart of Job is unrepentant and unmoved by Job's
plea of innocence in the eternal court of heaven. As if provoked by divine
will alone, God appears, and instead of answering the heart-born questions
of his servant Job, the Divine rises from the bench of eternal justice and
with the omnipotence of the Almighty charges the plaintiff with contempt
of court. Job having been lost in a sea of sorrow and regret, unaided in his
darkness or defense by blind counselors, had questioned the justice of the
unjust circumstances of life and incurred the anger of God. God appears and
humanity is condemned.

Job, who had known the greatest of humanity and been considered by some among their number, and who had been lost wondering in the realm of the righteous, finds himself when the light of God appears before him. Job's pleas provoked the presence of Providence, but when God appeared the perspective on Job's chaos and identity changed from terrestrial to celestial. And peering from the eternal view of God, Job's terrestrial terrors were negated by a divine revelation of himself. And in the light of God's understanding, he repented. Job despised himself when he saw his own image reflected in the light of God and his new opinion of himself shed a new light on his situation. Only then could order come to chaos and only then could he truly see and love God.

But woe unto to you . . . hypocrites! For you shut up the
kingdom of heaven . . .
Matthew 23:13

Actors at the altar of the Almighty sacrifice their souls and accumulate the utter distain of the Divine. Their piety purloins the flesh of men and women, unaware that their minds are trapdoors to hell and their hearts vacuous voids.

Jesus didn't have his biggest problem with those identified as sinners. The harlots, tax collectors, Roman soldiers, and the like who enter and exit the Gospel do so with Christ's kindest words and greatest blessings. His biggest problem was with the religious. Here in Matthew, Jesus gives a warning and sharp rebuke to the equivalent of our Sunday school teachers, Pastors, and church officers. He says their hypocrisy is an open and obvious discouragement to those who need God most. The sin of these well-intentioned thoroughly religious folk was their focus. They were overly concerned with how they looked and were esteemed, because they saw themselves in the mirror of public perception. So they carved out a pedestal in the community and guarded their perch against all and any that would expose or remove them. But this focus on themselves blinded them to a view of God and obstructed the light and love of God from all those around them. Their lust for power or position, their need for the esteem of others, their confidence in their own interpretations and understandings worked in their heart like a cancer, until with their eyes open they could not recognize God as he appeared in their midst. While diligent in their religious work, they ultimately despised an eternity with God and encouraged others to turn away.

Such men and women are in all churches, either chairing or comprising the key boards, some even perched behind the sacred desk; but beware of them for they are the beautiful portals to the regions of hell.

*As the shepherd takes out of the mouth of the lion two legs
or a piece of the ear, so shall the children of Israel be . . .*
Amos 3:12

It requires neither clairvoyance nor great powers of divination to declare the end of America. Black and brown children of the poor are incarcerated into cesspools of abuse and violence and placed in drug-induced stupors by imported parcels of white powdered hopelessness. Their lives and imaginations erupt as their living organs are expulsed in the pagan death rites enacted on the altars of American idolatry. But this is not the end of America, it is the rejuvenation of the genocidal slave-state that made this land the bastion of white hegemony it is. It is the resurgence of the darkness that looms greater than the lies within America's history. It is the shadow of darkness in the valley of death that bodes ill and beckons disaster. There need be no prophet to declare the coming terror, only a turn from the light of licentious religion to a perilous peering into the dark reality of today.

Amos appears from the southern farm fields of Tekoa to rail against the apostasy of the north. Those in Israel, who had grown rich managing the market economy of their ancient world, those who leveraged the labor of the poor on the backs of hungry children, those who lavished themselves with imported silks and satins, those living in comfort and joy are blind to God's perspective of their impoverishing wealth and vile oblations. So God sends the prophet to announce to those at ease in Zion, that God is insulted at the sound of their praise and provoked to anger by the sight of their sacrifices.

There is a perspective from the bottom of America that provokes prayers of justice. There is a balance in the hand of God in which we have been weighed and found wanting. The paradox for Christians on or allied with the bottom of American society is enjoining the peace of the Lord while enduring depredation.

*Let not my Lord regard this man . . . for Fool is his name
and foolishness is with him.*
1 Samuel 25:25

The fool cannot relate the bounty he enjoys with the toil of those who produced it or the God who provided it. In fact, the fool is convinced that he deserves the good he receives and that those without similar blessings are so because they do not deserve them. But the mind of a fool is not reserved to those with material possessions. Many without wealth are also fools because they believe in and justify the excessive wealth of others by lusting after excessive wealth themselves.

The wealthy Nabal celebrated the shearing of his sheep by sponsoring a party fit for a king, with him being the special guest. The past season had somehow spared his flocks and herds their usual attrition from bandits and beasts. And when the flocks were fleeced the weight of their wool witnessed to the abundance of the year's blessings, so Nabal rejoiced. Nabal believed he had only himself to thank and drank himself drunk in self-congratulatory praise. David hears of the feast his neighbor is throwing and sends an emissary asking if Nabal's kindness would extend an invitation to him and his men. Nabal rebuffs him and no invitation is given. When David hears Nabal's answer, he and his men remove the celebratory garments and put on their armor en route to kill, maim, and take what was not offered. But the warrior is intercepted by Nabal's wife, who provided for David and his men and thereby saved the life of her husband. Nabal hears of his wife's generosity and becomes enraged. But his unjust rage causes a heart attack. Nabal was ignorant of the hard work and suffering his own laborers produced or the protection provided by David because he chose to be blind to his blessings and deaf to the story of his deliverance. He was a fool because he discounted the preservation afforded him by those who worked for him and she who loved him. So when confronted with the truth, he refused to believe in it; in ignorance, his heart died.

The Hebrew word Nabal means fool. The story teaches us that the fool rests on the hard work and labor of the nameless and faceless masses and is unaware of the extent to which he depends on both the benevolence and patience of those very people. Nabal lived off the life of others, preying like a leech on the sacrifice of another's charity. But such a life killed his heart and his body soon followed. Beware of those with dead hearts; do not follow them for they are fools.

Hear, O Israel: The Lord our God is one Lord
Deuteronomy 6:4

Before you can love God you must hear. Before you can hear you must listen. Before you can listen you must be quiet.

When Jesus was asked by one who knew the law of Moses and the requirements of the Jewish faith which was the most important commandment, He replied "Thou shall love the Lord thy God with all your heart, with all your soul and with all your mind." These words were familiar to all worshiping Jews long before Jesus repeated them. They come from the heart of the Shema, which for many is the heart of all monotheistic religions. The Shema has been recited by faithful Jews for thousands of years—when they arose in the morning and when they lay down at night. It centers the believer on the essential task of mortal existence and reaffirms their relationship with God. But before the heart of Shema is revealed, before the imperative is recounted or imparted, it is introduced with its prerequisite, Listen Israel the Lord is God and the Lord alone. This preamble to life's imperative is vital, for without it all are incapable of fulfilling or even understanding the commandments that follow. By stating that the Lord is one, it affirms that God rules alone and places the petitioner at the final appellate, the highest and ultimate court. And by reminding the one in prayer that the Lord is God, it confirms that the

Lord who hears this prayer has the power and prerogative to answer. But most importantly, the Shema informs that one cannot love the Lord, understand that He reigns supreme or has all power, until one listens.

If we are to appropriate the blessing that comes with knowing and obeying God, we must first come to the end of ourselves. When we understand that we are not the final judge of our lives or that we do not have total control of our destiny, and when we stop the noise of our minds and the chatter of our mouths, only then have we positioned ourselves to love the Lord our God with all our heart, mind, and strength. The Psalmist says, "Be still and know that I am God."

*And David's men said to him, Behold, we are afraid here
in Judah: how much more then if we come to Keilah
against the armies of the Philistines?*
1 Samuel 23:3

The army of the Lord seeks for those who have strayed but is no har-bor for those who would run away. Heaven is a sanctuary for the misfits and malcontents of the world and a harbor for those in debt, but only if these same are willing to be changed.

David had risen from the small sheepfold of his father's flock to become a general in the army of Saul. With success came popularity and the young women of Israel began to sing his praise. The prophet Samuel had secretly anointed David to become the next king and all seemed to be going well, until Saul began to see him as the enemy. Saul then determined to destroy his rival. Now, David, though the heir to the throne, had to flee into the wilderness and hilly wastelands of Palestine. There he lived, a fugitive, hiding from place to place. While in their hideouts, the disenfranchised and the discontented gathered themselves to David, hoping for greater prosperity under the new chief. When the time came to fight the Philistines, those who had fled one set of circumstances desired to avoid the next, but they found out that they could not run away from the unkind forces of life. David's task was to disciple these runaways and misfits into a fighting army. They had to learn how to face their problems, to stand up and fight and conquer them. David had to learn how to make soldiers of sheep. Neither David nor the people with him were afforded the luxury of resting until their enemy perished. While in the wilderness, David developed character and the people with him gained courage.

God welcomes all who are weary and worn only to teach them to worship. God gathers the misfits of the world only to fashion them into the army of his kingdom. What God has for you, you will receive in time, whether you keep it or not depends upon the character and courage you develop while you are in the wilderness waiting for it.

Alas my master! How shall we do?
2 Kings 6:15

We serve a God of hope. Not that God and hope are synonymous or that the Divine is motivated by some innate desire to want what is not or to need what cannot be. God does not sit in the bleachers of eternity with his fingers crossed rooting for the mortals to make it. The hope of God is the ability to appropriate, possess, and use the Divine power and presence in our mortal lives. The hope of God is the access we have to sight, which renders our reality irrelevant. The hope of God is the ability to release the power of God into our lives and circumstances in spite of the powerlessness of our person.

The servant of the prophet, Elisha, woke early in the morning to begin the daily tasks of serving the man of God. He went up on the city walls perhaps to check the horizon for some hint of the day's weather and was dismayed and frightened by what he saw. During the night, the king of Syria had sent a large contingent of soldiers and chariots to lay siege to the city and capture the prophet. And the morning light found an alien army surrounding the city arrayed for battle. It was an intimidating sight and a foreboding reality. Alarmed the servant returned quickly to Elisha with the news. But Elisha was unmoved and unimpressed by the hopeless reality being related by his co-laborer. Elisha tells him don't be afraid, that there are more with us then are against us. Elisha then turns to God and asks God to open his servant's eyes so he can see beyond the hopeless reality. The Lord opens his eyes and he sees the mountains filled with the army of God mounted on horses and chariots of fire surrounding the Syrian army which surrounded the city.

We must not allow the fear that comes because of an awareness of our inability or a vision of potential chaos blind us to the abilities of God. Hopelessness is a gift from heaven when it is the precursor to confidence in God. Scenes that encourage us to despair are invitations to access the immutable power of Divine hope.

A certain man said unto him, Lord I will follow you
wherever you go.
Luke 9:57

Heaven is the home of those who have become homeless for the cause of Christ. The kingdom of God is the community of those who have estranged themselves from family and friends to wander the fields and streets of the world in the name of Jesus (and for the sake of the kingdom of God). To do less is to abandon the hope of heaven and sell your eternal soul for the ashes of the earth.

In the close of Luke's ninth chapter we are given the essential elements of three conversations with the Master. In the first, someone comes to Jesus and pledges to follow him wherever. But Jesus, who knows the heart of all, exposes the Achilles heel of the potential follower by explaining that he has no home, bed, or roof to guarantee. Next Jesus chooses one whom he would like to share company and asks this person to follow him; but He is asked if he would first be allowed to bury his father. Finally, the last requests the privilege of following the Lord after he says goodbye to his family. To each the Lord cautions the futility of what appears to be benign, if not reasonable, requests. The answer to the third person and epilogue of the text is that no one placing their hand on the plow and looking back is fit for the kingdom.

This is an unreasonable and illogical requirement. It is a violent prescription for the conduct of life. Yet this requirement to be cut off from the love and support of the familiar, untethered from one's base, now alien to the conduct of Christianity, is its foundation. Christ left the holy. Abraham left Ur. Moses left Pharaoh. Hannah left Samuel. And we are invited to no less commitment to the cross. The call of Christ requires a reckless abandonment of everything and every one except Christ. There are few so committed. These are they who have challenged the world and ordered our history. They are those who have prayed open heaven and closed the jaws of hell. They, and perhaps only they, are those who will live with Jesus.

Though he slay me, yet will I trust in him:
But I will maintain my own ways before Him.
Job 13:15

There are tests and trials of life that will strand you alone on the isle of doubt. There will be times for the believer when heaven harms and the earth rebukes. In such times, you will have only your integrity and that only before God.

Job sits bereft of all he cared for surrounded by his closest friends. The friends of Job have come to his side because they were true friends and, like Job, they were lovers of God in word and deed. The travesty of the week before was so complete and so troubling that they sat together in silence for seven days and nights. Job breaks the silence by cursing the day he was born. Job was convinced that never to have lived at all would have been better than to have lived, loved, and suffered such loss. This despair of life was as close as Job would get to blaming God for the disasters that destroyed his family and fortune. But for Job's dear friends who loved God even more than their great love for their friend, this despair was too close to blasphemy. They began to rebuke their friend and, defending the righteousness of God, they preached his justice to the condemned. Job had borne his sufferings well until this added burden of rebuke broke the damn that had held the flood of his questions in the sea of silence. He was unsure of heaven's motives but positive that he had done all he knew to do. He did not understand the sentence of the high court and knew only that he was not guilty. His closest friends, in an effort to defend the indefensible God, had no recourse but to apply blame and shame on their companion. So Job rises to release his anguish and declares that he will stand before God alone.

Job turns from his friends to the God who has already harmed him. He stands alone and aware of his utter need of an independent God. We are what we are and can be understood only by God. As Shakespeare wrote, "To thyne own self be true . . ."

Nevertheless we made our prayer unto our God, and set a
watch against them day and night.
Nehemiah 4:9

Never confuse prayer with hiding. Prayer is not an act of cowardice but a proactive and strategic move of empowerment to accomplish what you already understand to be the will of God. Prayer is an offensive act of a living and growing faith and is always an offense to the adversary of our souls. Neither is prayer the singular act of supplication, but prayer is the precursor and partner of acts of faith which it predicates and produces in the heart and hands of the supplicant.

Nehemiah and the families of faith have applied themselves to the rebuilding of the city of God and their fathers. They have each left the pleasures and complacency of exile and brought their feet and hands to their beliefs and have begun the restorative work of Jerusalem. As they begin the work, the opposition rises to be recognized and ridicules the project. Then when the laborers achieve progress and complete half the wall, the enemies of their good work coalesce their opposition and send word of their impending attack. The weary workers fall to their knees and pray. Surely as they knelt to pray, bending their sore backs in contrition, they felt the shadow of hopelessness peer over their shoulders. But before they would allow themselves to be embittered by the cold breeze of doubt they would stoke the fires of prayer to warm their souls. But they did not rise refreshed from the communion with God and ignorant of their new responsibility. Rather, emboldened by prayer they worked and watched day and night. Prepared by prayer they resigned themselves to the impending attack. Prayer empowered them to hold the helping hand of God and go on with the work God had ordained.

Prayer is not to be the crutch against catastrophe but the cloister from which we arise prepared to persevere in God's cause.

That we also may be like the other nations; and that our king may judge us, and go out before us, and fight our battles.
1 Samuel 8:20

We are slaves to what our eyes perceive, no matter how false or painful. It is a strange human proclivity to be attracted to and to paint pictures with our imaginations—images that will result in our persecution even as we hope otherwise.

The prophet Samuel has grown old. He has dispensed justice throughout the region with fairness and impartiality. His life was lived faithful to God and in benefit to the community in which he was both minister and prophet; on this all people agreed. Unfortunately, like Eli before him, Samuel had failed to raise sons who walked in his integrity, and the seer himself could not see that his own sons lacked substance. Perhaps love blinded Samuel. Perhaps a sense that God would change them in time motivated his faith in them. Samuel saw his sons as his hope and thought them capable of continuing his ministry, but the people saw them otherwise. So they demanded a king, but the prophet thought it better to entrust matters of succession to God's will. Samuel had succeeded Eli through Divine intervention, and the prophet thought, perhaps, God would eventually intervene again. But the people had a solution of their own: "Give us a king like all the other nations." Samuel tried to reason with them. He told them; a king would take their children as employees for his own use and purposes; he would expropriate their land, tax them to excess, and exasperate their every hope. But all the people could see was that a king would lead them in battle, represent them in the conflicts with the surrounding city-states, and be a symbol from which they could attribute status to themselves.

Samuel wanted to see his sons as worthy of his love and hope. The people wanted to see a king as their leader, deliverer, and salvation. But our lives are not fairy tales nor are our hopes sufficient to manifest into reality our unexamined dreams and desires. The success of our future is determined by a clear sighted and divinely guided confrontation with the present. God's picture of the present is often not pretty, but we must engage today's battles rather than exchanging them for faith in fantasies.

And He saw them toiling in rowing . . .
and would have passed them by.
Mark 6:48

There are those who too often want credit for how hard they work instead of for what they accomplish. We labor until the perspiration causes us to pause and then look heavenward for some sign of appreciation. We work wholeheartedly on half-baked ideas that don't accomplish anything, and we are disappointed when the angels don't sing our praise.

Jesus was on the mountain but could see his disciples toiling in the midst of the sea. He had told them to get into the vessel and precede him to the other side. But the storm winds impeded them in their attempt to obey. The disciples had begun their task in earnest but were thwarted by the powerful and unrelenting opposition. Jesus, aware of their struggle, heads in their direction. The waves and whipping sea pose no barrier. The density of the sea's surface strengthens to his will as he walks. The Master has performed miracles to arrive at the distressed disciples and would have passed them by had they not cried out.

When we begin to do as the Lord commands us, we are wise to expect opposition. Here the opposition was strong enough to stop the progress of the disciples completely. The task changed from moving forward in the will of the Lord to an attempt to maintain the progress they made. And as their fears mount and their hope descends, Jesus appears but is available if only they call him.

If Jesus would have come directly to their aid, it would have been an argument for mediocrity. It would have been a tacit endorsement that read, "Just try and I'll do the rest." By almost passing them by Jesus declares that trying is not enough. It was to declare that the work Christ gives us to do must be done regardless of any opposition, but that this same work can only be done by enlisting the aid and power of Christ. God is not impressed with what we try to accomplish without Him. Our inabilities are opportunities to realize first God's presence then Divine ability.

The eye of the Lord is upon them that fear him.
Psalm 33:18

We pour our confidence into ourselves as a child pours water into a linen sack. Often the more mature we grow, the more confident we become in ourselves. But neither the knowledge of things nor the experiences of a lifetime can prepare us for the tests of tomorrow or guarantee our victory today.

The Psalmist tells us that God looks from heaven and considers the imaginations of the human heart and the power of the human hand. Through this psalm the Almighty reminds us of the vanity of our self-confidence. The most popular ruler of the mightiest nation is as susceptible to the common cold as the pauper and as vulnerable to vain praise as the dog. The strongest soldier is too weak to lift his own spirits when they fall. Our mightiest machines make us no safer. We cannot stop the clouds from gathering, nor call rain down from the sky. We cannot by our wisdom prevent the tears we cry. Our loves are too little to last. Our peace is too particular to prevail. Our purpose is too paltry to preserve us. But the eye of God is upon them that fear him.

When God places the Divine eye upon us, we are delivered from death. When God places his attention on us, we are guided along the path of life and the plains of our own soul. When God places his eye upon us, the course of our life continues along corridors of conscious correction and we progress without digression. When God's eye is upon us, we are nurtured through the nonsense of nuisance. When God's eye is upon us, we are protected through the perverse particulars of our mortality.

To hope in God is to replace the confidence we have in ourselves with the hope that God's controlling eye is upon us. To hold on to God is to let go of the vanity of our temporality and yearn for the glance of the Almighty. Let your eye, oh God, be upon us until our eyes can see you as you are.

For we through the Spirit wait for the hope
of righteousness by faith
Galatians 5:5

For those whose hope is the Kingdom of God the failure of the flesh is a threat. Not because there is any sin great enough or debase enough to extinguish the power of Christ's resurrection, but because our sin tempts us to doubt the power of Christ's cross and turn from it to our own works.

Having been won to the kingdom of heaven through the knowledge of the death, burial, and resurrection of Jesus, the Galatians have turned back to placing their confidence in the law. Paul's pupils in the gospel accepted the grace of God, which redeemed them from the curse of the law and freed them to righteousness. But after the departure of Paul who brought them to faith they turned from trusting in the work of God in Christ to their own ability. Their inability to live up to their own expectations disappointed them to the extent that they rejected the grace of God. Because they were not holy enough for each other, they returned to the tables of self-righteousness and away from God.

When our minds and manic memories condemn us for the desires we have and have had, when our own hands betray us by working the misdeeds of the moment, we are tempted to curse ourselves with more restrictive rules and more punitive punishments. We prescribe for ourselves a renewed law with double curses and triple condemnation. But grace purchased us when we did not struggle against our depravity, and when we turn from it we deny the wisdom of God for choosing us, the knowledge of God who saw that we would fail, and the power of God that could save us without us.

We sin because we are still waiting and hoping for the righteousness of Christ to perfect itself in us. Our salvation is the faith through which we understand that God's grace is more powerful than our failures.

*I have likened the image of the daughter of Zion to a
beautiful and delicate woman. The Shepherds with their
flocks shall come to her, they shall pitch their tents
against her surrounding her, they shall feed everyone in his place.*
Jeremiah 6:2-3

We are not served by having the coarse edges of scripture sanded into smooth and pristine phrases conducive to our present notions of Christian piety. The translators and editors of our English Bible were empowered, like those before them, to transform coarse and violent phrases into more palatable prose. Yet, God is not more sanctified or honored by translations which hide the hard words of Divine wrath. For when we soften the words of the Almighty, we have at the same instant censured God.

The hopes of the small city-states of Judah were gone, her deliverer absent. Yet she imagined herself to be the crown jewel of Yaweh's eyes. The vassal kings of Judah continuously rebelled against their overlords, motivated by a confusion that convinced them to hope for an autonomy, which would lead to ultimate hegemony. But here Jeremiah's caustic admonition against such acts has been smoothed into irrelevance. The phrases of Jeremiah here imply a debase and malevolent act. Jeremiah is saying, Judah is like a princess arrayed in beauty and adorned in finery unaware that she is about to be objectified and raped repeatedly by the field hands of foreigners.

Are we better off remaining unaware of the depth of this simile? Have the translators helped us understand the danger of the godless arrogance of a nation or its leaders? To think of one's self being raped as a result of disobeying the will of God or the word of God's prophet is to come to grips with the depravity of disobedience and the consequence of corrupt Christian conduct. To be unaware of the Bible's naked vulgarity is to water down the text and undermine its truth. Hiding its plain speech renders it less assessable to the people of the land to whom it belongs and places it in an imaginary and secluded place. It is an ignominious act.

*And the younger of them said to his father, Father give me
the portion of goods that fall to me . . .*
Luke 15:12

Only a loving parent that has heard the biting tongue of a wayward child can understand the depth of the prodigal's action and the father's pain. It is only after you have held the nursing child to your breasts, after you have walked the night floors rocking their teary eyes to sleep; it is only after you have poured the waters of your life and hope into your child, holding them through the years in loving and selfless embraces, that you can fully understand the price of love. To hear your child reject all you hoped for them to be and all you hoped for them to have, to feel the cold distance in their voice as they speak to you as if you were a stranger is to begin to understand the love of God.

The prodigal, self-confident and ignorant of the world, demands of his father more than money or goods, for in his haste to enter the world the prodigal takes from his father the joy of parenthood and replaces it with travesty. The parable is used by Jesus to explain his missionary work among the so-called sinners and also highlights the depth of pain God experiences on behalf of the lost. Jesus explains that the Father does not only seek those that are lost, like the woman who lost her coin or the shepherd who lost his sheep. Jesus says through this painting that God grieves. A lost coin is an irksome annoyance easily replaced and of no ultimate value. A lost sheep is a sorrow and hardship. It is a damage to one's reputation and a threat to one's ability to survive. But the parable of the prodigal speaks of a wound that cuts to the soul, a harm and hurt unimaginable by all except those who have felt its grip.

To love is to provide the keys of your deepest treasure into the hands of a stranger. But Jesus offers this hope: the child will come home and the joy of the love returned will eclipse the pain of the love lost.

And David answered the priest and said to him, truly
women have been kept from us about these three days,
and the vessels of the young men are holy.
1 Samuel 21:5

There is a struggle between our natural desires and God's will for us. To engorge the flesh is to starve the spirit. Fleshly desires that are fed are never satisfied, rather they grow stronger until they possess our soul and every waking moment. God reserves the right to withhold anything, which would not be received as a precious gift from his hand.

David had fled the madness of Saul's murderous mind. He and his men arrive at the doorpost of the temple of God hungry and tired. They have the power to take what pleases them but instead they ask Ahimelek, the priest, for his benevolent care. The priest informs them that the only food available is the holy morsels which belong to God. David argues on behalf of his men for the gift of life that these morsels would bring and Ahimelek agrees to grant his desire with one precondition: that the men have kept themselves from women.

There is a point at which engaging the desires of the flesh corrupt our ability to access the blessings of God. When we request life or any of its necessary accouterments from the God of heaven it must never be a caviler prayer. In the tests that stress our lives we look either to satisfy our spirit or our flesh; whichever we feed will grow. If the men had recently engaged in satisfying their carnality, then they were not hungry enough to take from the feet of God. If the men were truly in dire need and poor constraints, they would have had little desire for the desserts of human relationships. And only if they were in dire need would they be ready to receive so holy and precious a gift from the table of God. We must nurture our flesh like the careful gardener giving enough but never too much; pruning, weeding and caring for it lest we allow the little lusts to choke our spirit and deny us the bread of heaven.

For I am a man under authority, having soldiers under me . . .
Matthew 8:9

Each of us commands an army. We engage our forces in pitched battles in order to protect our bodies, preserve our souls, and secure our salvation. Every imagination of our mind is a potential strategy, every hope of our heart is a possible objective, and every word from our mouth a deployed and un-recallable soldier en route to an objective. We deploy our forces upon the battlefields of our lives and either win or lose the silent, unseen conflict for our eternal soul.

Jesus is entering Capernaum on his way to Peter's house. As he enters the city, a Roman soldier intercepts him and begins to beg Jesus to heal one of his servant-slaves who was suffering greatly. Jesus offers to go to the soldier's home and heal the man. Whereupon the Roman declares that neither he nor his home is worthy of Jesus' presence, and he begs Jesus instead to send his spoken word to the house. His logic arises from his experience and his faith. As a Roman soldier in authority, he knew that the effectiveness of the world's greatest army at the time was a result of soldiers obeying the orders of those in command. He believed that the power of Jesus' forces were greater than the power of the illness that tormented his servant, and he engaged his faith by asking Jesus to apply that power and heal him. Jesus offers to delay his rest and change his course to address the Roman's plea when the soldier asks only that the words be sent. The soldier asks Jesus to give the order knowing that the force of Jesus' words will accomplish as much as Jesus' presence. Jesus marvels and applauds this man's faith, declaring it to be the greatest example of faith he had seen and sends the healing word.

Our words are the weapons in the warfare of life. They have the power to heal or destroy. Each of us with the authority to speak has the responsibility to select the thoughts from which we will send our words. We order our words, then our words order our lives.

Who darkens counsel by words without knowledge?
Job 38:2

We cannot grow in understanding by thinking of ourselves. The notion that the essence of humanity, the meaning of our lives, or even the substance of our character can be explored through the contemplation of our actions and ideas is not supported by God. It is only when we lose ourselves in others and sink our hearts in the soil and the soul of the earth that we have any hope of finding the who, what, and why of our being.

The contentious counsel of Eliphaz, Bildad, and Zophar made matters worse for Job and added mental anguish to his already tortured soul. Energy that Job should have applied to heal his broken heart was used to defend his person and assuage the hurt and negate the harm of his friends. His friends were as true as loving Godly friends could be, but they believed that by reasoning together they would find the hidden truth of God. All were involved in this tedious and temporal dance to the music of the human mind except Elihu. Elihu turns the attention solely on the person, prerogative, and providence of God, and when all the wise men are silent the Almighty speaks. And when God enters as the light that illumines their darkness God does so without regard to the substance or integrity of their argument or persons. God enters as God and exposes the penury of their logic and debauchery of their wisdom by expanding their view. God begins to expose them to the mysteries of the universe where there are obvious, grand, and important elements of their existence, which they had neither contemplated nor questioned.

By doing so God enlightens us in a manner that suggests we cannot know ourselves until we examine ourselves in light of the wonders of the world around us. We can no more understand ourselves apart from the universe God has made than the gene can understand itself apart from the living human being.

Peter took Jesus aside and told him to stop talking like that . . .
Mark 8:32

It is contrary to human nature to like bad news. Professional sports teams that loose often have the fewest fans. Politicians who suffer in the polls are abandoned by their constituents. Our classrooms initiate this behavior early in life with tests and grades, with pictures that get put up on the classroom walls, and pictures that don't. The earliest lessons of our lives convince us to live for the good and, at all costs, avoid the bad.

Jesus began an intimate conversation with his disciples with the question, "Who do people believe me to be?" The disciples answer with a variety of responses. Then Christ asks, "Who do you think I am?" Where upon Peter answers, "You are the Messiah." With this answer Jesus began to teach the disciples that he would soon be rejected by the elders, chief priests, and scribes, which would result in his suffering and death, but that he would rise on the third day. This compendium of bad news must have unsettled the disciples. It must have been very difficult to hear that the one they believed to be the promised of God would be rejected by the very ones who were thought to be the watchmen waiting for him. Surely the elders, priests, and scribes will come to accept the miracles and prophecies and raise Jesus to his rightful place. Perhaps the disciples and Peter preferred to be hopeful. Perhaps they preferred to believe that in the world all things are possible. In any case, they did not welcome the dower projection. So Peter took Jesus aside privately to correct him. Jesus noticed the other disciples were listening, and he rebuked Peter with harshness and clarity that still stings as one reads it: "Get away from me Satan; you don't want what God wants."

The good news of the Gospel exists only because of the bad news of the Crucifixion. God designs failure, rejection, and pain into our lives for God's own good reason. Hard times help those who by obedience are following the path God has chosen for them.

Why is it that you can see the speck in your brother's eye
and not perceive the log that is in your own?
Luke 6:41

The inability to forgive is a cancer which arises from unjustified and overactive pride. It is the result of not recognizing the overwhelming and outstanding debt you owe while holding over another their sins and short-comings.

In this chapter of Luke, Jesus is in the midst of laying an exact course to the Kingdom of God. While presenting a list of prescriptions for social interactions within the faith community, he turns the truth toward self inspection. He paints with his words a beautifully funny cartoon of a person with a large log in his eye attempting to remove a spec of dust from the eye of another. The absurd picture must have caused smiles if not outright laughter. Seeing or hearing the truth about ourselves in a way that does not condemn us allows us to smile at our shortcomings while we hope to improve. Then after Jesus had broken through the self-protective shell we create by dismissing all of our questionable actions, he reveals the sharp truth of his image. Often when we imagine or see a fault in another's character we are ignoring a greater flaw in ourselves. Jesus asks that we, who can hold microscopic inspections of another's life, instead make a macro correction of our own. Our flaws alone must be the focus of our corrective actions and intentions.

Each of us, whether we think our misdeeds small or great, have earned through our sin eternal separation from God. The grace of God transferred our debt to Calvary. The demonic cruelty exacted on his body and the separation from the Father, which incarceration in hell produced for Christ, was due us. We therefore owe an overwhelming debt of love and thanksgiving to God. Our continuing reliance on grace in light of our continued failures must realize for us an outstanding debt to love and forgive those others for whom Christ also died. Pride blinds us to our great debts and this is the blindness that leads to hell.

*That I may know him, and the power or his resurrection
and the fellowship of his sufferings.*
Philippians 3:10

Those filling the seats of our sanctuaries may mistakenly believe that they have fulfilled the request of the Gospel when in fact they have ignored the requirement of the resurrection. Something significant and irrevocable happened in the hearts and minds of the post-resurrection believers. Their knowledge of Christ so fundamentally changed their reality that their own lives and deaths were irrelevant compared to obeying Christ's command and communicating the truth of the resurrection.

Paul in his letter to the Philippians briefly recounted his history in an effort to demonstrate his abandonment to the Gospel. He recounts that his life prior to his encounter with Christ was complete with religious experience and exercise. He was actively engaged in what he understood to be the demands of piety. But something happened when he was confronted by the risen Christ that voided his every investment in his past religious expressions. Paul, with his conversion to Christ, began a journey in pursuit of an obedience that resulted in his being beaten, stoned, shipwrecked, falsely accused, abandoned, and more. Still Paul is desperate for a relationship with Christ that is deeper. Paul exposes his longing to know, believe, and experience Christ with a veracity and integrity that is beyond the pedigree of his earlier life or the perils and pain of his present experience. This embodies the requirement the first-century church understood. The triumph of the risen Christ provoked an understanding in the hearts and lives of the believers, which began a journey through danger and death.

These early believers were not content with pew sitting. Their righteousness was not merely right thinking. They were actively in pursuit of a redemption many take for granted today. Something about their understanding of the person of the risen Christ gave birth in them a passion and understanding that one could only become like Christ by following and experiencing all Christ experienced . . . including the cross.

And there is none of you that are sorry for me
1 Samuel 22:8

There is no more unenviable state of a human soul than when it seeks the pity of others. The saddest state of the spirit is when self-pity destroys our God-given strength and dictates our discourse and orders our interactions. Such a state renders us victims before the battle begins. The act of self-pity is a disempowering energy, which turns ourselves and those around us toward our destruction.

Saul had been anointed the first king of Israel by its most revered prophet and judge, Samuel. Samuel was informed by God that Saul was God's choice for the first king of the nation. Samuel anointed Saul and communed with him privately regarding the will of God. Soon after, at the time of the public selection and anointing service, Saul hid trying to avoid the call of God upon his life. When he was found, and when the people saw that he stood in their midst head and shoulders taller than the rest, the people shouted in joy and confidence for their new judge, deliverer, and King. But Saul's physical stature was much greater than his spiritual substance and his outer mass was no indicator of his inner strength. His initial hiding indicated his inability to move into the uncomfortable. Unwilling to grow and unable to accept who God had called him to be, Saul shirked from his responsibilities and sank from his opportunities. Until finally the anointed and appointed King is found lost in self-pity and pouting about his problems, unaware that they emanate from his own person.

Saul got addicted to the praise of the people and never fully allied himself with the will of God. His sails were driven by the winds of circumstance, so he shipwrecked and sank in the sea of self-pity. God calls us to hope in hopeless situations and to follow faithfully when fear is a more reasonable response. We must believe ourselves to be who God says we are and demonstrate God's image of ourselves to ourselves and others, always.

Jesus answered and said "I tell you for certain that even
before Abraham was, I am."
John 8:58

The purpose of faith is for you to have arrived before you get to where you are going. Accepting as reality that which is yet to manifest releases the pressure that builds from the tension of not being what one hopes to become or where one hopes to be. The ability to appropriate being from God through faith empowers becoming. It allows the universe to reorder itself according to the image God has placed in you.

Jesus stands in the midst of his harshest critics and has inspired their angst with clear statements of his dominion and authority. The moment arrives after Jesus has avoided a trap and delivered a woman from those who would have her killed, merely to impugn the love and compassion that Jesus demonstrated. Immediately after the incident Jesus proclaims that he alone is the light of the world and that God is his Father. The adversaries' tactics move from entrapment to indictment. The confrontation is sharp. The leaders ask, "Who are you?" as they question Jesus' parentage. Ignoring their insult, Jesus speaks to those who believed in him, assuring them that if they continue to obey him they will know the truth and be free. This widens the distance between those with Jesus and those against him. The leaders likely sensing the crowds movement toward Jesus and away from them, reassert their legitimacy and this time vulgarly insult the Master's; "We are Abraham's children you are the product of fornication." Jesus informs them that they are the children of the devil. The confrontation ends with Jesus narrowly avoiding being stoned to death by the leaders.

Jesus was the Savior before Calvary's cross or the resurrection. He was the Messiah independent of the acceptance of the religious leaders or the public. His faith in himself preceded our faith in him. His obedience to his Father and this faith is how we come to know him for who he always has been. Our life of obedience is the art of becoming, which allows us to be recognized as the one we have always known ourselves to be.

You have not resisted unto blood striving against sin . . .
Hebrews 12:4

Our three-month-old son had just been bathed and I laid him on the changing table to diaper and dress him. As I moisturized his skin and diapered him, he began to fidget and fuss; it was his way of telling me what I already knew, that he was tired and ready to be put to sleep. His fussing became crying and soon his crying became rage and screams. He had reached his limits; he could no longer bare the pain of his discomfort. He demanded that something be done that instant. I continued carefully to dress him taking no shortcuts even to tying the little shoes in which he could not yet walk. I then picked up my screaming child and brought him into the kitchen, where his bottle was already prepared. As he took his bottle he nestled into my arms and began to rest and sleep, all within four minutes.

The writer of Hebrews comments from his personal experience and knowledge of his initial reader. No one has beaten you bloody or killed you on account of your faith in Jesus. The writer reminds them and us of our Lord Jesus who endured the pain, suffering, and humiliation of the cross for the joy that was before him. He asks us not to be wearied or weak-minded in regard to our own high calling but like our Lord suffer for righteousness sake.

God prepares a table before us in the presence of our enemies and we get exasperated and angry because the service is too slow. Let us pray to grow up in our faith so that we are not children. Let us learn to endure with patience the tiny crosses of our lives, if for no other reason than to model for our children and others who in their lives may have greater burdens to bear than we.

I was not in safety, neither had I rest, neither was I quiet;
yet trouble came.
Job 3:26

The engine of a lost life is powered by fear. Many of us are driven to plot a deliberate course through life, which avoids that which we fear most or know too well. The child raised in poverty, given half an opportunity, will live an adult life achieving or lusting after financial gain. One raised in want will spend their life accumulating material possessions to excess. Yet no amount of financial success or material gain satisfies these same lost seekers. In fact, pursuit of their lusts leave them consumed by want or empty with plenty. But for some God places impassible obstacles along the road of life, detours which are designed to lead those who are God's to the true hope of their souls.

Job was a believer who was upright and as righteous as humanly possible. The Bible introduces him with the same admiration it gave to Noah; Job was a righteous man who pushed evil far from his presence. We have every reason to believe that Job was a deliberate and diligent worker. He had amassed wealth yet remained genuinely devoted to the Divine. While his adult children were vacationing and feasting, Job was sacrificing on their behalf. Job was one who did more than the minimum and took care of more than was required.

Yet for all of Job's work and piety, the thing he feared most, that which he worked hardest to prevent and avoid, came upon him. In one day he lost all of his earthly riches, his children, and soon after his good health. Bible readers learn what Job never knew, that God invited Satan to destroy all for which Job had worked. God illuminated Job to the darkness and its prince consumed all in view.

Job learned in one day what his book has been teaching for thousands of years; running from your fears strengthens them. To overcome your fears you must face them and hold on to life until they fall away.

Now when the adversaries of Judah and Benjamin heard
that the children of captivity built the Temple . . .
Ezra 4:1

To befriend and build on behalf of history and in hope of peace is to invite threats of war. To advance the cause of Christ is to provoke opposition. The walk of Christ is not a journey for the timid. Even seasoned Christians are caught by surprise when they become the enemies of others because they are following what they believe is the will of God.

Of all the Jews who were in Babylon less than twenty-five percent repatriated. Many of the Babylonian exiles of Israel remained in the homes and communities they had created in the strange new land. But the path to the Messiah continued through those few who returned to the fallow fields of their mothers and fathers. But as they sought to rebuild their homes and the temple of God, adversaries rose up against their good work. Enemies are never stronger than when they are working beside us. The first request of those who didn't want to see the temple built was to be allowed to help in its construction. They knew that from there they could slow and sabotage the building, discourage the workers, and undermine the will of God. But unable to join the workers, they next tried to influence those who influenced them and thereby accomplish the same destructive work. Finally, they appealed to a power greater than their own in hope that another might succeed where they have failed.

Expect opposition and adversaries when you begin to build your character from one level of faithfulness to the next. Expect opposition when you begin to build or rebuild your spiritual household. Expect opposition when God calls you to bring your work into a place where God could dwell. And when oppositions rise to the will of God, never falter and never fail; keep your eye on the goals of God for your life and muster the courage to face opposition and defeat it.

For I am ready not to be bound only but also to die at Jerusalem for the name of the Lord Jesus.
Acts 21:13

It is incorrect to assume or believe that living for Jesus will not put us in peril of our lives. "Take up your cross and follow me" is the invitation to death we must accept if we seek communion with Christ or care about our responsibility to him. It is dangerous to forget that long before the rock of resurrection there is the journey to and the passage through Calvary.

Paul had already proven his love for Jesus. He had taken up his cross on the Damascus road and followed Christ. He had been given the mission of preaching the good news to the gentiles, and for his obedience he left his home and family to wander the pagan regions of the Roman realm. He had been hungry, beaten, left for dead, and imprisoned. All this to obey the call to service he received from Christ in that blinding encounter. And here he stands after a full life of service and sacrifice, ready to die following the will of God for him. Notice that the Christians around him understood the peril. They prophesied the imprisonment and begged him not to do what he knew God wanted him to do. We cannot know the difference it made in the Kingdom of God when Paul walked in this obedience. Perhaps not even Paul himself fully realized the impact and import of his obedience. He only knew two things: that Christians prophesied danger and that the Lord commanded him to go. Of these two only one was important; to follow the commandment of the Lord.

This is the life of a believer. We are called to lay aside every weight, every lust to live and run with patience the race that is set before us. And the greater our victories of the past, the more difficult our challenges will be in the future. If we perish, we perish.

And he stripped off his clothes and prophesied before
Samuel . . . and lay down naked all that day and all that night.
1 Samuel 19:24

Either of two sins defeat our effectiveness and imprison us in an obsession with the irrelevant; either we are corrupted and confused by more activities than are reasonable or we are consumed by a single passion. The first divides our energies until they are of no eternal effect. The other pervades our soul and purloins our very lives.

The anointed and appointed King of Israel has become so obsessed with the death of an individual that he lost all other focus. There was little more important to Saul than his perception of the voice of the crowd. Saul lived as if he were unaware of the appointment of God or the anointing of God's prophet. Instead of leading the nation by listening to and relying on the word of God, whispered in his heart and hopes, he lusted after and relied on the adulation of the crowd. And when the women started to sing of the exploits of war, the Davidic melodies that once soothed his heart now provoked his wrath. Saul throws his javelin across his relationships to slay the mischievous musician and his own son-in-law, but David escapes. Saul's jealousy grows through hatred, to obsession. The chieftain then seeks to snatch David from the arms of his daughter and slay him in his bed, only to find he has fled to the prophet. Saul personally chases David to the sanctuary of Samuel. His sole focus was to kill David and perhaps Samuel and, if necessary, on Holy ground. He arrives to assuage his passion but the Spirit of God possesses him, and instead he prophesies and lies naked on the ground. Instead of affecting his will on the innocent and unarmed, he lies in open ridicule before the eyes of the crowd from whom he so much desired approval.

If we are not deliberate about what and why we believe, we may fall into the snare of myopia and loose perspective on the nature of our life and the relevance of our circumstances. To serve God is to be made aware of the greatness of God in you. It is to know that no one can accomplish God's will through you but you. It is to believe in your greatness because of the God that is with you. And at the same moment to serve God is to walk consistently in honest understanding of your utter unworthiness.

It is easier for a camel to go through the eye of a needle
than for a rich man to enter into the kingdom of God.
Mark 10:25

The rich are evil. When the disciples heard this thought from the lips of our Lord, they were astonished and found it too difficult to believe. So Jesus reaffirmed his meaning and restated this truth, "To be rich is to be exempt from heaven." These statements followed when Jesus met a rich young ruler and instructed him to go and sell all he had, giving it to the poor. Only then, Jesus commanded, would the young ruler be fit for heaven's service. The scene, the words, the reality was too much for the disciples to receive. They could not comprehend that what they had learned all their lives and heard all their days was not true. What was the fruit of all their labors is now declared by the Master to be worthless.

It is a marvel that the unwitting poor are offended by remarks, which expose the depravity of the rich. Most of us are paupers. If you beg for scraps along the highway hoping for a helping hand from your fellow man, you are a pauper. If you work as the means of your livelihood and are handsomely paid for your services, you are a pauper. There is only a slight degree of difference between yourself and the jobless. Today no one is more aware of the tenuousness of vocation than those who work for a living. But the poor have been duped into believing that, except for their lack of money and resources, they and the rich above them are the same. But the rich do not consider themselves the same as the poor. The rich view the poor as beasts. To the rich, the poor are dogs fit for nothing more than to labor at their overlord's requirement. The feasts of the poor consist of mere scraps from the table of wealth. Jesus declares that the rich are substantively and significantly different than the rest of humanity.

Opulence is predicated on penury. To create wealth is to impoverish. Therefore, the harbor of heaven is reserved for the poor. The rich will inherit the fires of hell.

Surely it is meet to be said unto God,
I have borne, I will not offend.
                Job 34:31

We have no right to receive reward for our work. God is neither obligated by justice or grace to bless us in life. Those who would be counted worthy of God's gaze bear the burdens of their lives silent to the pain. The gates of heaven swing on the hinges of a child's love and innocence.

The younger of the counselors of Job begins to speak only after his elder's have ceased. He dutifully rehearses the arguments of both sides, communicating the fact that he had been attentive, and then completely changes the focus of their inquiry. Job and the other friends had focused on Job. Their questions centered on Job's actions or inactions. Even though they assumed God's righteousness and defended God's justice, they argued as if humanity was of consequence to the Divine. But Elihu turned the conversation on its head. His focus was on the Almighty. Elihu spoke not on behalf of God but solely in praise of God, and as he focused on God the distance between God's prerogative and man's initiative grew greatly. No longer was the inquiry concerned with what Job had done or deserved, but it became an investigation of who God was.

When the center of the debate shifts from our thoughts of ourselves and our reflections on others to a contemplation of the identity of God, justice is consumed by omniscience and human righteousness is overruled by omnipotence. Such a focus on God produces a healthy disregard of our temporality. This is what led Elihu to understand and pray: "I have borne the burden of chaos and circumstance, I have endured the difficulty of humanity, I have tasted the terror of tortured pain . . . but I have no argument with the Almighty." Elihu brought Job back to the center from which he had strayed. For it was Job that taught Elihu with the words, "Though he slay me yet will I serve him."

My God, My God, why hast thou forsaken me?
Psalm 22:1

I despair of life so often and so easily. It is not so much over the tragedies of life: when some great horror hits the whole of my humanity, in such
times I find strength to persevere. It is in the mundane that the most profane
despair seeks possession of my soul. It is the little foxes, a tiny catalyst like an
untidy house, a dent in the fender, a cold or toothache, that brings me to the
brink of hopelessness. It is the benign betrayals of those I let close that lead
me to the brim of despair. It is then I feel most alone. It is then I feel bereft
of friend and abandoned by God.

"My God, my God, why have you forsaken me?" We read this verse and
images of our crucified Savior and Easter fill our minds. Seldom do we realize
that some believer before Calvary's cross was so bereft of life and so mired in
the pit of despair that these words were penned. Someone—David, Solomon,
a priest in Babylon, a peasant in the besieged Jerusalem—someone, somewhere
felt the pain inflicted by the unkind and unjust circumstances that invade
the human experience, and gave voice to this lament. Hopelessness is born
through the labor pains of loneliness and there is a sorrow of the soul, which
seeps through the vicissitudes of life and abandons us, if only for an eternal

moment, on an island of purposeless pain. And in such a state someone penned this Psalm.

And out of the writer's pain the Master of our souls, our God and deliverer, found hope in horror as he recited its verses at Calvary. Perhaps our pain can be used by God to ease the hurt of heaven. Maybe the pulses of despair that pass through our lives are the disguised yearnings for our home in heaven.

Rejoice you Gentiles with his people.
Romans 15:10

The outsider has always been inside God's plan. We all have a way of walking past, looking over, or otherwise disregarding the humanity of those who are not exactly like us. We allow insignificant distinctions, like the color of our eyes, the pronunciation of our words, or the texture of our hair, dictate our allegiances. We sanctimoniously endorse our evil imaginations of race, creeds, and gender into theological towers on the walls of our prejudice and live in the protected ignorance outside the will, wonder, and fullness of God.

Israel declined from the egalitarian-minded and mixed multitude that left Egypt. The prophets record that the pride, greed, and avarice of ancient Israel's socioeconomics resulted in a multi-tiered, racially segregated, and class conscious state. The prophets lamented the extent to which Israel mirrored the worst of those nations around her and reflected little of the God who birthed her through the Red Sea. They decried their disobedience, and not even the Diaspora healed their hearts. And here, after a thousand years of unreasonable pride, Paul speaks not to the insiders but to those thought lost and on the outside.

In these passages, Paul points out how the scriptures have long revealed that God was no respecter of persons. In fact, Paul shows here that the plan of Providence includes those on the outskirts of life. Most have in some way felt the sting of alienation at sometime in their lives. Most have been an outsider at some time. And those of us relegated to ignominy on the periphery of society—the homeless and the poor—the gentiles of the prevailing mythological notions of race, cast, or class must learn to rejoice because God has made provision for us in the Kingdom. We who are counted by them as not among them can rejoice with them because God has included us with God and God's people.

Are you the one who should come or
should we look for someone else?
Luke 7:19

W e doubt the power of the presence of Jesus when problems arise. Our perception of our situation or the reality of our persecution declares to the core of our being that Jesus has left us or, worse, is indifferent to our slow demise.

There was one who recognized Jesus while the Lord was still in the womb. John the Baptist began life in communion and cooperation with the plan of God and the witness of Christ. He grew up under vows of purity and centered himself and his ministry on the will of God. He was the prophet spoken about in Malachi who would turn the hearts of the fathers toward the children and proclaim the great and terrible day of the Lord. This John baptized the masses as they came to him in the Jordan. Even Jesus, in obedience to the Father, inaugurated his public ministry by being baptized in the Jordan under John's ministry. But suffering preceded John's public ministry and trouble followed. He learned and grew in the barren wilderness, eating locus and honey and lived in ignominy. Then when his public ministry began, he incurred the brunt of the political state when he commented on the inappropriateness of Herod's marriage. And now John, the obedient prophet of the coming Messiah, finds himself imprisoned and in danger. This is when John sends his disciples to the Master to ask Jesus the question. But the scriptures are clear that John knew who Jesus was. Perhaps John asks to be informed of what Jesus is doing because the impinging circumstances provoked doubt. Two things must have been clear: first, that he had done and said the correct things and second, that he was receiving unjust incarceration because of them. Jesus responds to the question by demonstrating that the Kingdom of God continues to be preached and expanded with power, a message that the Messiah knew the messenger would understand, even as he languished toward his death . . .

Our lives are not barometers of God's intention. Trouble in our circumstances is no clear indication of trouble in the plan of God. In fact, God designs predicaments and persecutions to protect and perfect God's image in us, and they are independent of but complimentary to the conduct of the Kingdom.

*For the Lord had returned the wickedness of Nabal
upon his own head.
1 Samuel 25:39*

Only those without wealth believe that wealth will bring joy and happiness. Peering across the avenue of circumstance, many imagine that to replace poverty with fortune would answer their soul's desire. Those who are assumed wealthy are presumed fortunate, but the perspective from a distance can blind. It is possible that those who have the wealth, which others could only imagine, live lives of unimaginable emptiness and sorrow.

Nabal, unaware of the deliverance his wife had purchased for him, drank himself drunk. His harvest was in, his sheep were sheared, and the tally of the bounty was so profitable that he held a feast in celebration of his fortune and in his own honor. Yet, the very act of numbing his mind with drinking was an admission of a sorrow and emptiness of his soul. His love of riches blinded him to the fact that his mistreatment and devaluation of others could only result in a devaluation and misuse of himself. He had begun long ago to hollow out his soul by longing for more food than his body could eat, more wine then his soul could drink, and more pleasures than his heart could hold. On the outside he was the envy of most, but the substance of his soul had long been sold, and he was as barren as the vacuum of space. He drank to fill the void that would not be filled. And after the silent pain, God replaces his unused heart with a stone and soon after his body dies and his soul sinks into unending torment.

Our lives must not consist of what we take and keep but of what we give and share. No one is richer than the one who by being friendly finds friends. No life is fuller then one lived laboring in the ground to give to others of your Godly gain. There is no greater vanity than to gather the fruit of another's labor in the garden of greed. Do not envy the rich; theirs is the burden of emptiness.

*And they did eat and drink before the Lord on that day
with great joy.*
1 Chronicles 29:22

Peace is the precursor to joy and joy is the overflow of a full cup on an
empty table. Peace is the smile generated by quiet contentment in the midst
of cacophonic chaos. It is a bath in a dry and thirsty land.

King David is presiding over the coronation of his son. The King, now
frail with age, has chosen the child of Bathsheba over the heir apparent. He has
selected Solomon, who had become a child of books and letters. Solomon did
not have the self-centered petulance of Amnon, the oldest of David's sons, or
the resolve and ambition of Absalom, who nearly snatched the kingdom out
of his father's hands. Solomon's life led him down another path. The wisdom,
for which he is later known, was formed in the silent years of his life at the
feet of his mother and in the sight of his father; but now he is King. And as
David places the royal crown on Solomon's head a thousand fires are lit upon
a thousand altars, and the people of Jerusalem begin to sacrifice and sing.
There is food in abundance to be eaten and drink without measure, and this
conjunction of circumstance and service to God has brought them to great
joy. Yet, in another part of Jerusalem, Solomon's elder brother Adonijah was
in the midst of his own coronation party. His self-appointed ascension to the

throne had been the precursor to Solomon's selection. And so in one day two sons laid public claim to the throne of their father; violence was sure to result. No nation can dwell in peace with two kings. But rather than retire to safe havens in hope of safety, the people eat and play in a celebration of great joy. Their deliberate communal service to God brought them into contact with the abundant provision of the Divine, even while aware of looming doom.

Joy overwhelms us when we deliberately decide to rest in the reality that God's provision and protection continues far beyond our sight or expectations. Joy is the ability to understand the presence and power of possible doom without yielding your peace or allowing even the smallest part of your confidence in God's provision to dissipate.

And Jesus asked him, saying, "What is thy name?" And he said,
Legion: because many devils were entered into him.
Luke 8:30

The mind is the synthesis of all it receives. Our emotions are but the reflections from this sea of thoughts, our words are pleas for paradigms of meaning from the paradox of confusion that the cacophony of information and experience bring continually to our doorstep . . . and how are we not mad?

The sandaled feet of Jesus touch the shores near the village of Gadara, and He is immediately met by one who has embraced the madness that can overcome any human; this man was unable to quiet the screams of the active mind. Matthew sees or hears two men, Mark and Luke report seeing only one man. Yet, whether there was one human being or two there is no doubt that before the healer stood a multitude of voices. The loudest of them all, it is recorded, shouted a plea for leniency from the recognized Son of God. But we know that here in this human frame there were also minions of evil capable of dark violence, for the villagers were terrified of the man. This madness must have also brought forces beyond human strength, for it is recorded that the man could not be restrained with either ropes or chains. So here before Jesus this man stands almost completely under the control and influence of a thousand powerful thoughts. And without any hint of unease at the confusion in front of him, Jesus speaks to the human being in the midst of the madness with a still small voice. The human being Christ seeks is almost lost to the oppression of screaming voices and barely recognizable. But Jesus is near and moves to separate the mind from the madness.

We walk on the brink of an insanity brought on by an inability to control, organize, and use the plethora of information and impulses we continually receive from memory and mind. We are sheep grazing in the meadows of our minds, each surrounded by a dark forest of fear, doubt, and oppression. We must cling to the voice of the Shepherd, for it is His voice alone that leads us from the dark dangers to sanity.